# Trinidad

Travel and Tourism, Business Environment.

Author
Godwin Kaur.

# Copyright Notice

Copyright © 2017 Global Print Digital
All Rights Reserved

Digital Management Copyright Notice. This Title is not in public domain, it is copyrighted to the original author, and being published by **Global Print Digital**. No other means of reproducing this title is accepted, and none of its content is editable, neither right to commercialize it is accepted, except with the consent of the author or authorized distributor. You must purchase this Title from a vendor who's right is given to sell it, other sources of purchase are not accepted, and accountable for an action against. We are happy that you understood, and being guided by these terms as you proceed. Thank you

First Printing: 2017.

**ISBN**: 978-1-912483-19-8

**Publisher**: Global Print Digital.
Arlington Row, Bibury, Cirencester GL7 5ND
Gloucester
United Kingdom.
Website: www.homeworkoffer.com

# Table of Content

Introduction ................................................................................................. 1
Past and Present ........................................................................................ 3
   *History* .................................................................................................... 3
      Trinidad ............................................................................................ 4
      Tobago .............................................................................................. 6
      British Control ................................................................................. 8
      Modern History ............................................................................... 9
      Crime .............................................................................................. 11
   *Culture* ................................................................................................. 12
      Events & Festivals ......................................................................... 19
      Trinidad's Natural & Built Heritage ............................................. 24
Economy .................................................................................................. 30
Tourism .................................................................................................... 33
   *Accommodation* .................................................................................. 33
      Eco Tourism ................................................................................... 37
      Hotels ............................................................................................. 39
   *Activities on Trinidad* ......................................................................... 51
      Diving ............................................................................................. 65
      Fishing ............................................................................................ 70
      Golf ................................................................................................. 72
      Nightlife ......................................................................................... 76
      Shopping ........................................................................................ 82
      Snorkeling ...................................................................................... 95
      Spas In Trinidad ............................................................................ 99
   *Attractions on Trinidad* .................................................................... 101
      Beaches on Trinidad ................................................................... 105
      Casinos ......................................................................................... 109
      Trinidad Landmarks .................................................................... 112
      Natural Attractions ..................................................................... 118
   *Cruising to Trinidad* ......................................................................... 126
   *Food on Trinidad* ............................................................................. 132
      Trinidadian Culinary Styles ........................................................ 136
      Restaurants on Trinidad ............................................................. 140
   *Maps Description of Trinidad* ......................................................... 145
   *Planning Your Vacation on Trinidad* .............................................. 150
      Booking your Trip to Trinidad .................................................... 151
      Budgeting .................................................................................... 155

- Getting Info ... 161
- Making Decisions ... 165
- Packing ... 168
- Best Time to Visit ... 173

*Transportation Options for Trinidad* ... *177*
- Trinidad Air Travel ... 181
- Buses on Trinidad ... 186
- Trinidad Ferries ... 188
- Trinidad Rental Cars ... 190
- Sailing & Boating ... 200
- Taxis on Trinidad ... 207

*Travel Basics* ... *212*
- Clothing ... 217
- Currency ... 219
- Customs ... 221
- Driving ... 226
- Electricity ... 228
- Embassies ... 229
- Health ... 238
- Hours of Operation ... 244
- Languages ... 245
- Passports ... 247
- Postal Services ... 249
- Telephones ... 254
- Time Zones ... 256
- Tipping ... 258
- Tourist Offices ... 260

*Weather on Trinidad* ... *262*

*Weddings on Trinidad* ... *265*
- Budgeting & Planning ... 271
- Locations & Venues ... 279
- Requirements & Traditions ... 286

*Why Not Go to Trinidad?* ... *289*

# Introduction

Some people are happiest in a fast-paced city with never-ending attractions that allow them to go, go, go; others prefer peace, quiet, and nature untouched by human hands. The dual island nation of Trinidad and Tobago is the perfect destination for either type of traveler, acting as the figurative "city mouse" and "country mouse" of the Caribbean.

Trinidad and Tobago is an archipelagic state in the North Atlantic Ocean in the Caribbean. It shares maritime boundaries with Barbados, Guyana, and Venezuela. The geography of Trinidad and Tobago includes mostly plains with some low mountains.

he government system is a parliamentary democracy; the chief of state is the president, and the head of government is the prime minister. Trinidad and Tobago has a mixed economic system in which there is a variety of private freedom, combined with centralized economic planning and government regulation. Trinidad and Tobago is a member of the Caribbean Community (CARICOM).

# Past and Present

Trinidad in the Past and in the Present
**Trinidad and Tobago are two islands with very different histories and cultures, united by politics**
The island of Trinidad has a unique history among Caribbean islands. Separated from its sister island of Tobago, the individual histories have led to differences between each of the islands and have created two distinct cultures.

# History

History of Trinidad
**Trinidad and Tobago have come together in recent years**
Columbus discovered Trinidad and claimed it for Spain. The island's native Indians were exported as slaves to mine gold in other Spanish territories, including Mexico. The island is located between the Caribbean Sea and North Atlantic Ocean, encompassing a total area of

1,841 square miles; over ninety-percent of the total Trinidad and Tobago nation.

Many European nations fought for the island, but the British walked away with Trinidad around the turn of the 19th century. Once under British control, Trinidad still remained separate from its Tobago neighbor. Today, Trinidad and Tobago share governmental responsibilities, under a bicameral republic. The President is the head of state, kept in check by the Parliament, which is headed by a Prime Minister.

The islands of Trinidad and Tobago, though now united as one nation, have had their own separate histories. The islands have changed hands many times over the years, and the two have been united politically for barely 100 years. Still, their unique histories do share some similarities.

## Trinidad

Columbus discovered the island of Trinidad in 1498 and claimed it for Spain. During this time, the Caribbean gold rush drew many Spanish sailors who exploited gold found in other colonies. Trinidad's lack of gold kept it from being settled immediately. Despite the Spanish claim on the island, they were not the first to own it.

Amerindian tribes known as the Carib and Arawak lived on the island before Columbus' time. It's not clear who dominated the population - the warlike Carib or peaceful Arawak - but it is believed that the majority of inhabitants were Arawak. Little was known about these native people because the Spanish used many of them as slaves. The discovery of ancient pottery and bone fragments beneath the parliament building during a renovation project in 2013 along with DNA testing of 25 members of the Santa Rosa First Peoples Community indicates that there is a link to Amerindian and African ancestry dating back to AD 0-350. These findings remain in the preliminary research phase, yet are still important to note.

Though the Spanish claimed Trinidad for some 300 years, they did not settle the island until late in their reign, at which point some were arguing to the Spanish crown for better treatment of the Amerindian natives. However, this did not halt the process of enslaving the Arawak. The island was not economically viable for settlement until 1718 when cocoa plants began producing crops. Problems with the 1733 crop returned Trinidad to anonymity.

With less than 800 inhabitants in 1772, Spain made an attempt to entice settlers to Trinidad to augment the population of 300 Spanish settlers. About 400 Amerindians still lived on the island, and many

French settlers were soon to join their ranks. Spain offered Catholic non-Spanish immigrants many incentives to immigrate to Trinidad. However, discrimination was still in place: Whites were offered twice as much land per person as non-whites, and those bringing in slaves were also granted a portion of land per slave. Immigrants were also forced to give their loyalty to the Spanish crown.

Just 25 years later the population had grown to more than 16,000, including 2,100 white Europeans and 4,500 free Africans. In 1797 the British took control of Trinidad from the Spanish, but they were left with the question of how to handle the large population of free blacks and few British settlers. Social and political pressures caused the British government to ban the importation of agricultural slaves to Trinidad.

## Tobago

Columbus sighted Tobago, but it was relatively ignored until the 17th century. Called Tobaco by its Arawak and Carib inhabitants, Columbus called it Assumption. The British claimed the island in 1626 and established Tobago's first colonial governing body. However, a great number of governments quickly began making claims to the island.

The Spanish invaded in 1636, worried about their settlements on Trinidad should the Caribs on Tobago form a coalition with the tribes on Trinidad. The Duchy of Courland, a Baltic state, was granted rights to the island in 1639. In 1646, both France and Holland claimed ownership of Tobago. The small country of Latvia claimed the island as a colony in 1664. France fought the Netherlands for control of Tobago and won decisively in 1678. Courland finally relinquished its claim to the island in 1690. Despite the large number of claims to the island, none of these countries ever truly settled Tobago.

The 1700s saw much fighting between the major powers, despite the fact that France and Britain agreed to the neutrality of Tobago in 1749. The neutrality was short-lived. France and Spain became allies in 1756 to go to war against Britain. At the end of the war, Tobago was a British territory.

France took the island back from the British in 1781 and offered incentives to colonists. Between 1771 and 1791 the island's population more than tripled to over 15,000, although 14,000 of the inhabitants were slaves. The end of the 18th century brought an end to the fighting over the island. In 1803 the British took Tobago from the French and have had control ever since.

## British Control

Once under British control, Trinidad became a Crown Colony. Britain granted the island this unique status due to the unusually high number of land-owning non-whites on the island. The status of Crown Colony denied residents the right to vote, keeping non-whites entirely out of the political process. Many of the white residents were not British, so few objections were raised.

British Emancipation in 1834 gave Tobago its own representative government, but did not help Tobago's economic problems. The metaire system was introduced in order to sustain the economy. Workers were not paid for their labor, but shared crop profits with the landowners. However, even this could not bolster the island's economy.

Trinidad was also impacted by the 1834 Emancipation. Prior to that, the ban on the importation of slaves made agricultural production difficult, but not impossible. Despite the labor shortage, sugar, cotton, cocoa, and coffee were farmed on Trinidad. Indentured servants from China didn't stay long because the males were relocated to the island without their family or any social support structures. And despite the ban, some slaves were smuggled into the island. Indian workers became indentured servants between 1845 and 1917.

In 1833, Tobago was united with Grenada, St. Vincent, and Barbados under the governorship of Barbados. At that time, Tobago was still stubbornly refusing to give up rights to Britain, but this dispute was eventually settled. Tobago's request for association with the island of Trinidad was granted in 1898. Tobago remained somewhat fiscally independent, and the Tobagoins argued for more independence. Britain eventually brought the two islands together both financially and politically.

Racial and class relations have influenced the political and social history of both islands and have been a strain on Trinidad especially. The collapse of the sugar industry throughout the West Indies in 1897 truly hurt the islands, and Trinidad and Tobago struggled economically as a result.

## Modern History

In 1910, Trinidad's world value changed when oil was discovered off the island's coast. Returns from the first World War also brought cultural changes, and by 1925 the people of Trinidad and Tobago received voting rights. Sugar production was almost nonexistent by 1929, but the oil industry bolstered the islands' economy.

Low quality of life in 1937 caused a sit-down strike, and 1946 brought the first universal suffrage election on Trinidad. The People's National Movement (PNM) led a political conference in 1956 that put forth a new political and social agenda, with goals to diversify and enlarge the economic base as well as fight for reform of island problems. Eric Williams, the leader of the PNM, kept control of the government for the next 20 years.

More social unrest arose in the early 1970s and the "February Revolution" brought thousands of workers and students into the streets. During the next 10 years, Trinidad and Tobago fought to establish international political and economic relationships with countries such as Cuba, China, and Russia.

In 1976, political and economic development spurred by the oil industry led to the decision to make Trinidad and Tobago an Independent Republic. The U.S. was the biggest trading partner with the islands in 1977. In 1981 Prime Minister Williams died, and in 1986 another political party, the National Alliance for Reconstruction, was voted into office.

In July 1990 a coup attempt on the islands' government caused some troubles, but the future is looking bright for Trinidad and Tobago. The economy is improving and the government is currently stable. While racial and class relations are not as smooth as they could be, the history of the islands has calmed down in recent years.

# Crime

## All About Crime on Trinidad
**Vacationers can avoid potential crime by taking a few precautions**
Trinidad and Tobago are generally safe places to visit, but crime has become a rising issue in recent years.

Most crimes committed on Trinidad than on Tobago are theft. Vacationers can protect themselves from becoming victims while on vacation by remembering a few safety tips.

- ➤ Theft can happen anywhere and any time.
- ➤ Travelers should not travel alone on deserted beaches and streets.
- ➤ Protect your belongings by storing valuables in safes, if available at your hotel, and by locking your hotel room doors when you leave.
- ➤ Always make sure you lock all doors when you park your rental vehicle.

> If your passport, birth certificate, or driver's license are stolen while you are on either island, immediately contact the local consulate or embassy office.

Drugs are not tolerated on the island, and vacationers should be aware that even a small amount of marijuana can lead to serious jail time.

One of the more serious concerns facing Trinidad and Tobago is the rise in gang related activity. This has become such an issue that the islands declared a state of emergency, which allowed the government to impose a curfew, which helped police officers to weed out criminal activity.

Gang violence is generally focused on rival gang members, and tourists have little to worry about. Still, before your vacation it is wise to check with the U.S. Department of State for important travel warnings and updates relating to criminal activity.

The islands of Trinidad and Tobago are beautiful and exciting places to vacation. Travelers can make the most of their time here by taking a few safety precautions to ensure a safe and unforgettable vacation.

## Culture

## The Culture of Trinidad
**The culture of Trinidad and Tobago is focused on music and carnival**

The culture of Trinidad has been the stronger of the two islands. Carnival originated on this island and spread to become one of the region's most famed cultural celebrations. This fun-loving lifestyle has dominated Trinidad, while Tobago is home to a more laid-back lifestyle.

Music has always gone hand-in-hand with Carnival celebrations, and is a truly important aspect of island culture. Calypso, soca, and other musical styles that have become popular throughout the country, even if they haven't made it to worldwide popularity, have played an important role historically, as well.

The islands of Trinidad and Tobago have two very different tones. Trinidad is the upbeat, fun island, while Tobago is more laid back. However, both have similar cultural backgrounds, and their rich cultures create a wonderful country to explore.

Music and festivals are the most dominant means of cultural expression here, but arts are also important to the culture. Carnival is the most well-known cultural festival, and calypso and steel band music are both internationally popular.

## Carnival

The annual celebration of Carnival takes place across the Caribbean, but it originated on the island of Trinidad. Each year just before Ash Wednesday, this festival fills the streets where vacationers and locals mingle to watch parades and celebrate. Don't be surprised if you're invited to play mas' (short for masquerade).

Partygoers wear brightly-colored costumes covered in sequins and feathers and spend their days dancing and partying in the streets. In fact, it's recommended that you sleep a little extra the day before Carnival if you plan to take part in the festivities.

The original Carnival celebration was only for the masses. Members of the island's upper class would watch, but not participate in the festival. The Carnival on Trinidad and Tobago has given rise to a number of recurring characters.

- Dame Lorraine is a well-endowed woman.
- Jab Jab looks like a devil who wears horns and carries a three-pronged pitchfork; he may threaten you, but all in fun.
- Pierrot Grenade is a character who speaks in rhyme on topical issues.
- Midnight Robber continues the tradition of the African Griot storyteller in his own "robber talk" dialect.

➢ Minstrels, black and white musicians in face paint, continue a tradition of the wandering minstrel.

## Carnival Music

Trinidad and Tobago has a great history of music, which has been strongly influenced by the music performed by the Africans brought to the islands as slaves. But, in 1883, the wildness of the Carnival celebrations caused drums - a main element on Trinidadian music - to be banned during the festival. This forced islanders to develop new ways to incorporate rhythm into their celebrations.

Tambour-bamboo was a way of playing on cut bamboo. A five-foot stick of bamboo was used to create a bass drum effect, while foot-long pieces were struck together by hand to create a counterpoint, called a foulé. The third piece of bamboo, called a cutter, was long and thin, and was struck by a piece of wood. The tambour-bamboo was also eventually banned; the style eventually faded and is rarely played now.

Steel band music replaced the tambour-bamboo style, and has become so popular that it is well-loved outside of Carnival as well. String music with a Spanish flair known as parang was imported from Venezuela. However, it is rarely played outside the two months before

Christmas. This style is most loved as an accompaniment to calypso singers among the upper classes.

The most recent addition to Carnival music is called Trinbagonian. This new genre blends African and Indian music together in a calypso and chutney mash-up that can be heard nowhere else on earth. Carnivals of late have been promoting the new sound by offering monetary rewards for the best use of the genre during the festival.

**Steel Band**

Developed in Port of Spain in the 1930s, steel band music, also called steel pan music, came from the steel oil drums. Though they were originally used only as drums as a part of Carnival celebrations, developed as an alternative to other banned rhythm instruments, the different sizes and parts of the drums were used to create different notes, making tuning a true skill. Musicians may be particularly interested to note that the steel pan claims the distinction of being the only non-electronic instrument created in the 20th century.

This instrument, however, was not well-received by the people of Trinidad and Tobago, because it was initially perceived as a musical form for the lower classes. It was not until the 1960s that this art form was truly recognized. Prime Minister Eric Williams encouraged corporate and business sponsorship of steel bands, which helped to give disadvantaged youth a means of self expression. In just over 10 years, Trinidad and Tobago saw the rise of some 200 steel bands, averaging 25 members apiece.

Like the tambour-bamboo, these steel band instruments came in three tones. Tenor pan carries the melody, the kittle provides the harmony, and the boom creates the rhythm. Additional pieces of the band are the double tenor pan, which plays the harmony alongside the melody of the regular tenor pan. The alto, guitar, and cello pan all create rhythm, while the bass pan and tenor bass pan both carry a bass line. Scratches are added with drum sets, and iron adds drum brakes.

**Calypso**

Calypso was particularly popular worldwide in the 1950s. This type of music is more about the words than the music, and the songs' prior uses included slave communication. Even now the West African word "kaiso" is occasionally used for calypso, as it is a truly African-derived form of music on the islands.

Calypso has become an important part of Carnival festivities as well. The Calypso Monarch and Road March King are two important titles earned by singers during carnival, and are often political, featuring social commentary and humor as well.

Soca, chutney soca, and rapso are three types of music that have spun off from the popularity of calypso. Soca offers more powerful rhythms and simpler lyrics. Soca with an Indian musical infusion is called chutney soca, and rap- infused soca is called rapso.

**Race and Religion**

One of the most unique aspects of the islands of Trinidad and Tobago is their unusual ethnic breakdown. While most Caribbean islands are populated in large majority by the descendants of African slaves, Trinidad and Tobago are home to many immigrants from the East Indies, who came to the islands as indentured servants after slavery was abolished in the 1800s. This gave Trinidad and Tobago a distinctive culture unlike any other island's as these cultures blended.

The following statistics were derived from the 2000 census:

| Ethnic Group | Percent of population |
| --- | --- |
| Indian (South Asian) | 40% |
| African | 37.5% |
| Mixed | 20.5% |
| Other | 1.2% |
| Unspecified | 0.8% |

Similarly, the religions practiced by Trinbagonians are unusual due to their mixed population:

| Religion | Percent of population |
| --- | --- |
| Roman Catholic | 26% |
| Hindu | 22.5% |
| Anglican | 7.8% |
| Baptist | 7.2% |
| Pentecostal | 6.8% |
| Other Christian | 5.8% |
| Muslim | 5.8% |
| Seventh Day Adventist | 4% |
| Other | 10.8% |

Though these are not the only cultural elements you'll find on Trinidad and Tobago, they are some of the most important aspects of the island culture. Remember that Carnival originated on Trinidad and Tobago, and its development has been important among the entire region, as have the many musical stylings associated with the festival.

## Events & Festivals

## Trinidad's Events and Festivals
**Celebrate the cultures of Trinidad and Tobago as one**

The people of Trinidad and Tobago are proud of their diverse heritage, and celebrate all that makes their island nation unique and they do it often. Chances are there will be a festival of some sort going on during your stay; whether it be cultural, musical, or athletic. Make plans to attend a street festival, listen to local music, or cheer on the winning yacht at a regatta.

## Cultural Celebrations

**Carnaval**

Carnaval is the Caribbean's premier cultural event, with over 40,000 visitors arriving on Trinidad and Tobago alone to celebrate the flashy event. In Trinidad and Tobago Carnaval is celebrated in February or March, and is a huge street party and cultural event. Attendants dance to soca and calypso music as they parade down main roads in tattered, sparkly clothing, feathered head dress, and other costumes that evoke images of a more lively masquerade ball. The event features a soca music competition, a steel pan band competition, the crowning of the Carnaval King and Queen, and a showcasing of ornately decorated Carnaval costumes (some are so extravagant that they weigh up to 200 lbs). Trinidad's version of Carnaval was voted as the Best Festival in by *Caribbean Travel + Life's* readers in the 2011

"Best of the Caribbean" awards, and *National Geographic*'s "Top 10 Pre-Lenten Celebrations."

**Emancipation Celebration:** Emancipation from slavery on Trinidad and Tobago became official on August 1, 1834, and this day is celebrated every August in Port of Spain. There are performances of both traditional and modern song and dance, plus booths with food and crafts.

**Tobago Heritage Festival:** In August, each village on Tobago puts on a dramatic or musical performance to honor the African heritage of the island.

**Diwali:** Diwali, also known as the Festival of Lights, is a national holiday that occurs in November. It is a Hindu celebration, though all denominations take part in the event. Many people wear East Indian clothing, there is much prayer, religious ceremony, performances, and lighting of deyahs.

Music Festivals

**Panorama Steel Pan Festival:** The Panorama Steel Pan Festival is the January celebration of Trinidad and Tobago's national instrument, the steel pan.

**Jazz Artists on the Greens:** Local jazz musicians put on a night of fine music each March on the lawn of the UWI Centre for the Creative and Festival Arts.

**Tobago Jazz Festival:** For eleven days at the end of April, Tobago hosts the Tobago Jazz Experience. Music lovers from around the world converge to hear the sounds of jazz, soca, Latin, R&B, world beat, and reggae. The event is so popular that airlines like Caribbean Airlines increases their domestic service capacity by about 35 percent.

**Tobago International Gospel Festival:** Celebrate the power of gospel music with a two-day event in June featuring performances by local gospel artists.

**San Fernando Jazz Festival:** In October, the San Fernando Jazz Festival takes place atop San Fernando Hill. Tickets cost between TT$200 and TT$350.

## Sporting Events

**Tobago Carnaval Race:** The Tobago Carnaval Race, held in February, features a series of regatta races, including Optimist and Bum Boat races, wind surfers, and kite boarders. The event is more than a chance to watch the races. On shore activities, such as a pig roast, bonfire, and on-shore games round out the party.

**Tobago International Game Fishing Tournament:** The Tobago International Game Fishing Tournament is held in Charlotteville each March. Anglers compete to catch the largest yellowfin tuna, blue and white marlin, wahoo, dolphin, and sailfish.

**Carib Great Race:** Expert sailors sail from Port-of-Spain to Crown Point every August, in the toughest power boat race in the Caribbean.

**Buccoo Goat and Crab Race Festival:** Annual 100-meter goat race and much shorter crab race held in April with much pomp and circumstance.

**Angostura Tobago Sail Week:** The Angostura Tobago Sail Week is a week of regatta races around Crown Point in May.

## Other Events and Festivals

**Great Fete Weekend:** Great Fete Weekend is known as the best beach party in the Caribbean. The five-day party takes place at Store Bay and features such themed days as Welcome Wednesday, Retro Active Thursday, Free Drinks Friday, Sandbox Wet Fete, and Breakfast Party Sunday.

**Taste T&T Festival/** Sample dishes made by some of Trinidad and Tobago's most inspiring chefs each May in Port-of-Spain.

This is just the beginning. Each month numerous events and festivals bring the streets of Trinidad and Tobago to life. As you explore the islands you are sure to hear talk of the upcoming celebrations. Make plans to take the time to attend one during your vacation; it will provide you with a real sense of what means the most to the islanders.

**Film & cinema**

The film industry has long been earmarked for growth, and incentive and rebate programmes have made the islands an attractive location for filming. Work by locally-based and Caribbean diaspora artists are on show at the annual T&T Film Festival (see our Festivals guide for 2017). Some home-grown features also get runs at local cinemas (the most popular of which are MovieTowne in Port of Spain, Chaguanas, and San Fernando; Caribbean Cinemas 8 in Trincity and San Fernando; and the Digicel Imax in Port of Spain). The UWI Campus Film Classics, Studio Film Club, and European Film Festival host special screenings of regional and foreign indie films

# Trinidad's Natural & Built Heritage

In between Trinidad's many modern buildings and ultra-contemporary homes, architectural gems peep out, legacies of Trinidad's many influences religious, social and economic. Among the most beautiful and appealing are the signature gingerbread houses, many Catholic churches and cathedrals, classic Islamic mosques, Hindu mandirs, 18th century mansions built by cocoa kings, former sugar plantation homes and museums, such as the National Museum and Art Gallery, which has a German Renaissance style.

For the history buff, there are a great many archaeological and historical sites in Trinidad and Tobago. Many are in the process of being protected and preserved by the National Trust, though there is still much work to be done in preserving our natural, cultural and built or achitectural heritage. A few sites require special permission to access (which can usually be done by an authorised tour guide).

## North Trinidad

The Magnificent Seven

A row of grand old houses on the western side of the Queen's Park Savannah, were built between 1900 and 1910. The most southerly is Queen's Royal College, whose most famous alumna is Nobel Prize-winning writer (and quintessential Trini) VS Naipaul. Hayes Court was the residence of the Anglican Bishop of Trinidad and Tobago and is still the property of the Anglican Church. It is currently under renovation. Next door is Mille Fleurs, which was built in 1904 for the Prada family. It was bought by the government in 1979, but has never been used, like many structures in this wealthy nation, and is now falling apart.

Roomor, originally known as Ambard's House, was commissioned by a cocoa merchant. It is the only one of the seven still functioning as a private residence. Just three doors down from the Anglican bishop's residence is the home of the Roman Catholic Archbishop of Port of Spain. The building has been renovated and is used by the church.

Whitehall was, until 2008, the office of the Prime Minister of Trinidad and Tobago since shortly after independence. It is still being renovated and restored with plans for it to be used as a Protocol House for visiting dignitaries.

The northernmost of the seven, Stollmeyer's Castle, was originally named Killarney. It remained the property of the Stollmeyer family until the 1970s and was eventually bought by the government in 1979. It too was scheduled for conversion to a Protocol House in 2008, along with White Hall; however, the work is still ongoing.

History buffs will find cannons and other relics scattered throughout the island. The gingerbread house has delicate wooden filigree, jalousie windows, peaked roofs, dormers and a gallery. George Brown, a Scottish architect who came to Trinidad in 1880, created the gingerbread style, which can be found across the island, in remnants of stately mansions once owned by planters and merchants, as well as the humble cottages of the working class.

More: Quite a few gingerbread houses can be seen in Woodbrook, the western suburb of Port of Spain that is now the liming hub of the country. A living museum of architecture, this former sugar estate became a respectable suburb for a new emerging middle class in the early 1900s. Belmont, to the east of the Queen's Park Savannah, has also held on to some of its beautiful old homes, which are in remarkably good condition.

## The National Museum and Art Gallery

Though not part of the Queen's Park Savannah's Magnificent Seven, the National Museum and Art Gallery is housed in a building of significance. Established as the Royal Victoria Institute, in honour of Queen Victoria's Diamond Jubilee, the building is an example of the German Renaissance architectural style. The more celebrated example of this style in Trinidad and no more than a stroll away from the museum is Queen's Royal College. The two buildings share a common architect: Daniel M. Hahn, an old boy of QRC, who received training in Germany. Today, the building houses both the national art collection and a history collection comprising artefacts from the country's earliest known Amerindian settlements to (almost) the present day.

*Two smaller museums in Port of Spain complement the main collection:*

The Museum of the City of Port of Spain: A collection designed to narrate the history of Trinidad's capital. Opening hours: Tuesday to Friday, 9am to 5pm. Fort San Andres, South Quay, Port of Spain (opposite City Gate bus terminal). Tel: 623 5941/624 6477/623 0339

Police Service Museum: There has been a Police Force in Trinidad since 1592, established by the Spanish. For its first two hundred years, however, it was never more than half-a-dozen strong. It is bigger, and busier, now. Opening hours: Tuesday to Thursday, 9am to 5pm; Saturday, 10am to 3pm. Old Police Headquarters, St Vincent St, Port of Spain. Tel: 624 6722.

## African Legacy Tours

These inspiring and educational tours take in sites of African heritage across the two islands. Africans were first brought here in 1606 to work on tobacco plantations. However, most came in 1783 with the plantation owners of islands that the French had claimed. Emancipation was proclaimed at the Treasury Building in Port of Spain by Governor George Hill on August 1, 1834; the freedom for which the Africans had ceaselessly fought was finally achieved four years later, on August 1, 1838.

The tours celebrate the rich legacy of the Africans, as well as the contributions of their descendants, to the heritage and culture of

Trinidad and Tobago. You will learn about their resistance, Maroonage, Pan Africanism and links to continental Africa, as well as their spirituality and ancient legends, new discoveries and modern heroes. Tel. 461-8637

**Emperor Valley Zoo**

Tigers, giraffes, lions, macaws and lots of snakes. Kids will love it. The young giraffes are adorable and the new lions and tigers are big draws. Get a good look at some of the many species of monkeys, parrots, macaws, snakes, fish and reptiles that inhabit the forests of this land. Open every day exept Christmas and carnival. Admission: Adults TT$30, children TT$15, 8am–5:30pm (weekdays) and 8am–6:00pm (weekends). www.zstt.org

# Economy

## The Economy of Trinidad

**Agriculture and oil have been important for the economy of Trinidad and Tobago**

While lacking large scale gold deposits commonly found in South America, Trinidad has something just as valuable; oil. This black gold has supported the island's economy for years. Agriculture, manufacturing, and tourism have also had a part in the country's economic development. Though the tourism industry plays a smaller role on Trinidad than it does on other Caribbean islands, it is still an important one. The nation boasts over 4 thousand hotel rooms, and sees over 200 thousand visitors each year during tourist season - a significant number of these guests arriving during Carnival.

Throughout the islands' relatively peaceful history, a distinct culture has developed. However, while Trinidad and Tobago are culturally rich, their economy is poor. In recent years the struggle has been toward a better life for island inhabitants. The tourism industry has helped to do this, and visitors can enjoy their vacation knowing that they are not only relaxing in a tropical paradise, but contributing to Trinidad and Tobago's economy as well.

Throughout history, the islands of Trinidad and Tobago have each been very different. Trinidad has been significantly agricultural, but recent years have brought much economic diversification. On the other hand, Tobago's economy has been almost entirely reliant upon agricultural products and fishing. Recent years, however, have introduced tourism to the economy.

Agriculture, especially sugarcane, coffee, cotton, and cocoa, was important to both islands. As a result, indentured servitude was also important to the economy of the islands once they were finally settled. In the 20th century, oil reserves were found off the coast of the islands, making a big difference in the local economy.

**Oil**

The 1970s were known for high worldwide oil prices. Fortunate for Trinidad and Tobago, oil was discovered off their coasts. These high prices created an economic boom, and the islands were able to rid themselves of financial debt and greatly improve their infrastructure. However, Trinidad and Tobago experienced troubles when oil prices dropped in the late 1970s.

Some speedy financial planning cut back public spending and development projects helped to avert an economic crisis. But these same cutbacks in the 80s and 90s caused a recession. But there is more than oil to the islands' economy.

**Tourism and More**

Surprisingly, tourism has not been a particularly important source of income for Trinidad and Tobago. Nonetheless, tourism has given the islands a minimal economic boost in recent years. The importance of tourism declined in the 1980s, but the number of vacationers have been rising in recent years.

Agriculture, manufacturing, and banking are also important on the islands. Manufacturing is important on many islands, and agriculture has, of course, declined since colonial times. Banking is minimally important, but has had hard times as well. One other source of income for Trinidad and Tobago has been yacht services, which are popular among visitors.

Due to their history, location, and unique natural traits, the islands of Trinidad and Tobago have struggled over the course of their economic history. However, they have been working toward much more economic stability in recent years.

# Tourism
## Accommodation
Trinidad Accommodation Options
**Travelers can find the right accommodations to match their vacationing needs**
On Trinidad, Port of Spain is where you will find many dining and shopping opportunities, as well as plenty of attractions to visit. There is also a great variety of lodging options in this area, from your typical hotel to rental properties. If you're looking for a more quiet beach atmosphere, Blanchisseuse is the better choice. Other places on the island known for hosting vacationers include Matelot and Chaguaramas.

**Hotels**

You will find a few categories of hotels to consider on the island, including a few bed & breakfasts and a variety of hotels. Travelers looking to enjoy a spirited bar scene will encounter exactly that at a pair hotels around Trinidad. Read further info regarding each property by clicking on them.

A popular spot for on-site recreation is Hilton Trinidad & Conference Centre. Featuring a beautiful view of the Gulf of Paria and the city of Port of Spain, the Hilton Trinidad guarantees guests, whether visiting for business or pleasure, an unforgettable vacation. With guest rooms featuring private balconies, a fitness center and sauna, outdoor pool and tennis courts, and 25 acres of landscaped gardens, each vacationer is treated to their own unique experience. They are located on Lady Young Road.

For those seeking to stay somewhere with a good late-night scene, Hyatt Regency Trinidad is one spot you may want to consider. There are over 400 guest rooms available at the Hyatt Regency Trinidad. All feature bamboo flooring, flat screen televisions, Grand Elegant Plush Hyatt beds, home stereo, and glass shower or baths. They're located on No.1 Wrightson Road.

Visitors who are in search of good on-site dining possibilities may want to look into The Carlton Savannah. A luxury boutique hotel, the Carlton Savannah is at once chic and accommodating, perfect for business travelers as well as those looking for a high-end retreat. Everything you need is taken care of and you'll never have to lift a finger when you stay at this stylish spot. You will find them at 2 Coblentz Avenue.

Needless to say, you can find a nice selection of options too. Read on Hotel page in this book.

## Camping and Eco-Tourism

Travelers who want to be close to nature should check out the selection of eco-tourist options offered to them on the island.

Guests looking to book their stay on Trinidad will enjoy accommodations like Laguna Mar Estate. The resort boasts two, six-bedroom guest lodges and a four-bedroom cottage for a variety of vacation needs. Each room is equipped with private bathrooms and balconies that take full advantage of the Trinidadian vistas. Visitors can find them at 12 Ramlogan Terrace.

Las Cuevas is a nice property on Trinidad. The rooms at Las Cuevas Beach Lodge are clean and comfortable, each with a private bathroom, television, and air conditioning plus views of the mountains and rain forests. The Premium Rooms have two queen beds, a small refrigerator, and a microwave oven. They're located on North Coast Road.

Nature lovers can find a selection of different eco-lodges on the island, including Asa Wright Nature Lodge. Each of the cottages available is cozy and comfortable decorated with modest furnishings and with private verandas where you can see the grounds of the Nature center right from your room. You can reach them at (800) 426-7781.

Of course, there are additional options too. Read on Eco Tourism page regarding these types of properties if you want to find some more facts.

## All-Inclusive Accommodations

Some travelers like the simplicity of paying for everything on a single bill. There are multiple explanations why these plans are successful. For example, they allow you to know what your vacation will cost before you go. The one option below is the only all-inclusive property available here.

Vacationers looking to book their stay on Trinidad should consider accommodations like Royal Palm Suite Hotel. Royal Palm Suite Hotel is a great locale for guests who are traveling on a budget, but don't want to compromise on lodgings. The rooms are kept comfortable and clean, the staff is friendly, and the view is worth writing home about. They're located at 7 Saddle Road.

All-inclusive lodgings offer food and other amenities for one flat price; however, other inclusions may vary. To avoid an unpleasant surprise, call ahead or carefully study the official website, to learn exactly what's included in the all-inclusive price.

# Eco Tourism

Trinidad Eco Tourism Lodging Options
**Unspoiled natural areas provide travelers with eco-adventures**
With large areas of unspoiled forests, slopes, and oceans, campers and eco-adventurers on Trinidad have rich and numerous opportunities to satisfy their thirst for nature and adventure. Whether taking in a rare species of bird, or mountain biking to a spectacular ocean view, travelers are sure to enjoy the ecology of the islands.

Although the waters at many of the beaches on Trinidad and Tobago are too rough for the average swimmer, the scenic views along the miles of unspoiled sands provide travelers with good options for camping. Many of the beaches have facilities helpful to campers such as parking, restrooms, and changing areas, and some may even have nearby food and drink vendors. Vessigny on Trinidad is an example of a beach that have established camping facilities available for use. Contact the Forestry Division on Trinidad and Tobago at 868-622-4521 or at 868-622-7476 when making your plans.

Other travelers may wish to hike and camp in one of Trinidad and Tobago's dense and lush rainforests. Guides are recommended here, and many adventure services and even some eco-adventure oriented hotels can offer guests guided hiking and camping tours. Many nature preserve areas, such as the Asa Wright Nature Centre, may have small eco-lodges or guest houses nearby. Accommodations in these areas can start as low as $25(USD) to $40(USD) for shared accommodations, and run from $60(USD) to $185(USD) per person for private accommodations during high season.

Even for those who are not interested in hiking or camping, Trinidad offers an abundance of wildlife and natural environments that anyone can enjoy. Bird watching is immensely popular on the islands, and Trinidad and Tobago are home to hundreds of species of unique and exotic birds. The Asa Wright Nature Centre and the Caroni Bird Sanctuary are both popular destinations for bird lovers. Tobago is a popular destination for both scuba divers and snorkelers with diverse fish and coral species coloring the ocean floor. Windsurfing, kayaking, mountain biking, and fishing are all popular as well. can be rented for as low as $7(USD) a day. Many adventure services will offer tours for hiking, biking, and bird watching.

The rich flora and fauna, both in the water and out, make Trinidad and Tobago prime areas for eco-adventurers who seek the thrill of experiencing new and diverse environments. Read our Guide to Nature on Trinidad for more information about the islands.

# Hotels

## Trinidad Hotels
**Direct access to detailed information about hotels on Trinidad**

Trinidad is renowned for being a prime destination for ecotourist pursuits such as scuba diving and, in particular, bird watching. Small posh beach resorts, eco-friendly inns, and business traveler hotels can all be found in locations ranging from Port of Spain to the rural interior.

Many people who visit Trinidad and Tobago consider Tobago to be the leader in quaility accommodations. However, you can also find luxury lodging on Trinidad, but travelers on a budget will find mostly moderately priced accommodations here. Just because you're paying less for your hotel doesn't mean you must forgo the little extras. Many mid-priced priced hotels and inns on both Trinidad and Tobago offer their guests pools, up-to-date décor, and fine food. These smaller hotels and resorts may not be as luxurious as the island's expensive rooms, but travelers will find that these accommodations can meet their budget as well as their lodging expectations.

Whatever style or size of hotel you choose, the bill will include a 15 percent government tax as well as a 10 percent service charge. Because of the limited amount of accommodations on Trinidad and Tobago, travelers visiting the islands during the week of carnival should secure their hotel or resort reservations months in advance to ensure availability.

## Hotels On Trinidad

There are multiple property types to select on the island, including a few bed & breakfasts and plenty of hotels. Those looking to enjoy a lively late-night scene will encounter exactly that at a pair hotels around Trinidad. Read additional information regarding each one by clicking the links.

One of the top choices on Trinidad to find a variety of on-site dining possibilities is The Carlton Savannah. Each with a kitchen, dining room, and laundry area, the 157 guestrooms turned 51 suites a nestled into lush gardens. The top three floors have Juliette balconies and black out curtains, and corporate executive as well as extended guests enjoy laundry, chauffeur, and butler services. Find them at 2 Coblentz Avenue.

For active travelers that enjoy partaking in various outdoor pursuits, Radisson Hotel Trinidad is one of those destinations that offers lots of recreational opportunities. With its waterfront location and close proximity to the heart of Port of Spain, the Capital Plaza Hotel Trinidad is an ideal destination for both business and leisure travelers. They are located on Wrightson Road.

Another notable option is Crews Inn. Set away from the busy areas of the island, Crews Inn is the perfect spot for sailors and anyone looking for a quiet, relaxed getaway. From the world-class dining to luxurious accommodations, and of course the expansive boatyard and marina. Visitors can reach them at (868) 634-4384.

Be sure to look at this table for details on hotels.

HOTELS ON TRINIDAD

| Name | Type | Phone Number | Star Rating | Location |
| --- | --- | --- | --- | --- |
| Ambassador Hotel | Hotel | (868) 628-9000 | | Downtown Port of Spain |
| Bel Air International Airport Hotel | Hotel | (868) 669-4771 | | 2.9 mi. West-Southwest of Central La Horquetta |
| Cara Suites Hotel And Conference Center | Hotel | (868) 659-2271 | | Claxton Bay, Central Trinidad |

| | | | |
|---|---|---|---|
| Cascadia Hotel And Conference Center | Hotel | (868) 623-3511 | 1.3 mi. North of Central Belmont |
| Chaconia Hotel | Hotel | (868) 628-0941 | 4.3 mi. North of Central downtown Port of Spain |
| Chancellor Hotel | Hotel | (868) 623-0883 | 1.8 mi. North of Downtown Port of Spain |
| Coblentz Inn Boutique Hotel | Hotel | (868) 621-0541 | 1.7 mi. North of Downtown Port of Spain |
| Courtyard by Marriott Port of Spain | Hotel | (868) 627-5555 | 1.7 mi. West-Northwest of Downtown Port of Spain |
| Crews Inn | Hotel | (868) 634-4384 | 0.5 mi. East-Southeast of Central Chaguaramas |
| Crosswinds Villa | B & B | (416) 785-0698 | 6.5 mi. Northeast of Central Port of Spain |
| Duke's Guest House | Hotel | (868) 222-4768 | Downtown Port of Spain |
| Forty Winks Inn | B & B | (868) 622-0484 | Downtown Port of Spain |
| Hilton Trinidad & Conference Centre | Hotel | (868) 624-3211 | 1.9 mi. Northeast of Downtown Port of Spain |
| Holiday Inn Express Suites Trincity | Hotel | (868) 669-6209 | 3.6 mi. East-Southeast of Central St. Augustine |
| Hotel Par May Las Inn | Hotel | (868) 628- | Downtown Port of Spain |

Trinidad

| Name | Type | Phone | Location |
|---|---|---|---|
| | | 2008 | |
| Hyatt Regency Trinidad | Hotel | 86-8-623-2222 | Downtown Port of Spain |
| Inn At 87 | B & B | (868) 622-4343 | Downtown Port of Spain |
| Kapok Hotel | Hotel | (868) 622-5765 | Downtown Port of Spain |
| L'Orchidee Boutique Hotel | Hotel | (868) 621-0618 | 1.6 mi. North of Downtown Port of Spain |
| Maracas Bay | Hotel | (868) 669-1914 | 0.3 mi. Northwest of Central Maracas Bay |
| Melbourne Inn Trinidad | Guest house | (868) 623-4006 | 0.9 mi. Northwest of Downtown Port of Spain |
| Monique's | Hotel | (868) 628-3334 | 3.0 mi. North-Northeast of Central Port of Spain |
| Normandie | Hotel | (868) 624-1181 ext. 4 | 1.7 mi. North of Downtown Port of Spain |
| Pax Guest House | Guest house | (868) 662-4084 | 1.4 mi. North of Central St. Augustine |
| Radisson Hotel Trinidad | Hotel | (868) 625-3366 | Downtown Port of Spain |
| Royal Palm Suite Hotel | Hotel | (868) 628-5086 | 2.5 mi. North-Northeast of Central Port of Spain |

| | | | |
|---|---|---|---|
| Sun Deck Suites | Hotel | (868) 622-9560 | 1.6 mi. East of Central Belmont |
| The Carlton Savannah | Hotel | (868) 621-5000 | Downtown Port of Spain |

If you would prefer having a wider variety of properties beyond the category here, you might want to expand your planning horizon. To reach our guide about other kinds of accommodations available for Trinidad, Read on Accommodation page.

At the opposite end of the spectrum are the islands' eco-friendly accommodations. Interested in hiking, camping, and other eco tourism options during your visit? There are plenty of choices for you as well.

## 5 Stars
### Trinidad and Tobago Hotels with 5 Stars
You will find plenty of variety among accommodations in Trinidad and Tobago, however, we have not currently rated any properties with 4.5 or 5 stars. For all of your other options, take a look at properties that have been given star rankings, or visit our alphabetical listing of all hotels and resorts on Trinidad and Tobago. You and your family are sure to spot something that fits your budget and your ta

## 4 Stars

## Trinidad and Tobago Hotels with 4 Stars

With lots of places to stay, from little cottages that have comfortable furnishings to large hotels with upscale facilities, Trinidad and Tobago makes for a diverse vacation destination. Hotels listed here have been given a rating of 3.5 or 4 stars. These hotels and resorts have the most plush surroundings and some of the region's best service, making for a pretty perfect experience.

Suites with incredible views, paired with outstanding service, are just a few reasons to enjoy Trinidad and Tobago's high-end hotels and resorts. With all the finest treatment you'd expect from a hotel with 3.5 or 4 stars, you can have any kind of vacation you desire.

These star ratings were created from a few different sources. They are derived from data provided by industry sources, interviews with hotel personnel, and hotel websites -- providing you with valuable insight well before you arrive. Seeing more information about the following hotels is easy. They're listed in alphabetical order, starting with the Hilton Trinidad & Conference Centre. Just click the name of a hotel and you can see detailed articles about what's in store.

4 STAR HOTELS ON TRINIDAD AND TOBAGO

| Hotel Name | Location | Tennis Court |
| --- | --- | --- |

| Hilton Trinidad & Conference Centre | 3.3 mi. East of Port of Spain, Trinidad | |
| --- | --- | --- |
| Hyatt Regency Trinidad | Downtown Port of Spain, Trinidad | |

## 3 Stars

## Trinidad and Tobago Hotels with 3 Stars

There are several different accommodations in Trinidad and Tobago, from cozy hideaways to spacious and comfortable suites. Hotels listed here are rated with 3 or 2.5 stars. Though they don't have flashy decor or expensive extras, these modest but well-appointed properties are a smarter choice for many families.

For travelers searching for well-maintained accommodations that doesn't have pricey amenities, hotels with a rating of 2.5 or 3 stars are probably the best places to start. However, affordability is not the only thing that makes them worth booking. Many people prefer the more laid-back and low-key charm that you can't always find at some of the upscale properties.

These star rankings were developed from a number of sources. They are based on data obtained from industry sources, personnel interviews, and hotel websites, allowing you to anticipate your accommodations before you arrive on Trinidad and Tobago. Learning more about the properties below is a breeze. They are ordered in alphabetical order, beginning with the Ambassador Hotel. Just click on any hotel and you can view detailed pages about the options it has in store.

3 STAR HOTELS ON TRINIDAD AND TOBAGO

| Hotel Name | Location | Tennis Court | Swimming Pool |
| --- | --- | --- | --- |
| Ambassador Hotel | Downtown Port of Spain, Trinidad | | |
| Cara Suites Hotel And Conference Center | Claxton Bay, Trinidad | | |
| Cascadia Hotel And Conference Center | 2.9 mi. Northeast of Port of Spain, Trinidad | | |
| Chaconia Hotel | Maraval, Trinidad | | |
| Coblentz Inn Boutique Hotel | Cascade, Trinidad | | |
| Courtyard by Marriott Port of Spain | 0.1 mi. Northeast of Port of Spain, Trinidad | | |
| Crews Inn | Chaguaramas, Trinidad | | |
| Forty Winks Inn | Downtown Port of Spain, Trinidad | | |
| Inn At 87 | Downtown Port of Spain, Trinidad | | |

| | | | |
|---|---|---|---|
| Kapok Hotel | Downtown Port of Spain, Trinidad | | |
| L'Orchidee Boutique Hotel | Cascade, Trinidad | | |
| Laguna Mar Estate | Blanchisseuse, Trinidad | | |
| Las Cuevas | 13.1 mi. Northeast of Port of Spain, Trinidad | | |
| Monique's | Maraval, Trinidad | | |
| Normandie | St. Ann's, Trinidad | | |
| Pax Guest House | 9.3 mi. North of Chaguanas, Trinidad | | |
| Radisson Hotel Trinidad | Downtown Port of Spain, Trinidad | | |
| The Carlton Savannah | Downtown Port of Spain, Trinidad | | |

## 2 Stars

Trinidad and Tobago Hotels with 2 Stars
With many lodging categories to choose from, from hotels with personal service to fabulous suites, Trinidad and Tobago appeals to all types of visitors. Those listed on this page have been given 1.5 or 2

stars. Though they don't have lavish rooms or fancy features, their reasonable price and great service draw in most types of visitors.

For visitors who want a nice experience without those extra, expensive frills, these hotels offer a good starting point. However, affordability is not the only reason that they're worth booking. Many prefer the more charming and authentic experience that you don't always get at some of the fancier resorts.

These star ratings were developed using information gathered from several sources. They are derived from data provided by industry sources, personnel interviews, and hotel websites, which help us evaluate what you can expect before you select a property. Learning about the hotels below is a breeze. They are listed in alphabetical order, beginning with the Asa Wright Nature Lodge. Just click the name of a property and you will be taken to a page dedicated to the details of everything it has to offer.

2 STAR HOTELS ON TRINIDAD AND TOBAGO

| Hotel Name | Location | Tennis Court | Swimming Pool |
|---|---|---|---|
| Asa Wright Nature Lodge | 15.2 mi. Northeast of Chaguanas, Trinidad | | |
| Chancellor Hotel | St. Ann's, Trinidad | | |

| | | |
|---|---|---|
| Crosswinds Villa | 6.5 mi. Northeast of Port of Spain, Trinidad | |
| Holiday Inn Express Suites Trincity | 7.6 mi. Northeast of Chaguanas, Trinidad | |
| Maracas Bay | Maracas Bay, Trinidad | |

## 1 Star

## Trinidad and Tobago Hotels with 1 Star

There are lots of lodgings in Trinidad and Tobago, from authentic inns to large and lavish resorts. The properties listed on this page have been rated with 1 star, or are not yet rated. While these hotels aren't the highest ranked in the area, they are a smart choice for travelers who don't plan to spend much time in their rooms anyway.

Though these hotels are not among the highest rated properties, or are not yet rated, they can provide an authentic experience for those traveling on a tight budget, particularly if you don't plan to spend much time at the hotel anyway. If you are the type of traveler to prefer something that's authentic, low-key, and won't put a strain on your wallet, these hotels offer a good starting point.

These ratings were created using research gathered from a number of sources. They are derived from data obtained from industry sources, interviews with hotel personnel, and hotel websites, letting you know what you should expect before arrival. Viewing information about any one of these properties is easy. They are ordered in alphabetical order, starting with the Bel Air International Airport Hotel. Just click on any hotel and you will be taken to our comprehensive articles about what it has to offer.

1 STAR HOTELS ON TRINIDAD AND TOBAGO

| Hotel Name | Location | Tennis Court | Swimming Pool |
|---|---|---|---|
| Bel Air International Airport Hotel | 6.6 mi. Northeast of Chaguanas, Trinidad | | |
| Duke's Guest House | Downtown Port of Spain, Trinidad | | |
| Hotel Par May Las Inn | Downtown Port of Spain, Trinidad | | |
| Melbourne Inn Trinidad | Woodbrook, Trinidad | | |
| Royal Palm Suite Hotel | 2.5 mi. North-Northeast of Port of Spain, Trinidad | | |
| Sun Deck Suites | 3.9 mi. East of Port of Spain, Trinidad | | |

# Activities on Trinidad

# Every vacationer can find something to interest them on Trinidad and Tobago

A trip to Trinidad and Tobago means you can sleep in late, spend your days lounging on the beaches, and your nights partying and having fun. Or, you can wake up with the sun, hit the links, take in the sites, and make sure not a moment is wasted. It's all about what you want to do on your vacation, and there is plenty to do.

## Diving

You'll find 7 dive operators to choose from. For a more thorough discussion of scuba diving in this area go to Diving page.

## Events and Festivals

As is true with spectator sports, the chances that an event or festival will occur during your trip to the islands is pretty great. The most popular festival of the year is Carnaval, which is celebrated throughout the Caribbean at different times. In Trinidad and Tobago the event takes place in February or March. Be sure to read on Events and Festivals page in this book.

## Fishing

Anglers will be pleased to know that every time of year is good time of year to get in a little fishing. Fishing tours are popular, or you can rent some fishing equipment at a tackle shop and cast a line at any beach.

If you like to go fishing you will be happy to know there are a few charter fishing services located in this area. Those needing to obtain more information concerning fishing in this area can do so reading on Fishing page in this book.

## Golf

Golfing is popular in this area, as suggested by the existence of 6 different golf courses. Some of the area courses include St. Andrews Golf Club, Millennium Lakes Golf & Country Club, and Pointe-a-Pierre Golf Club. For a detailed guide to the course all you have to do is click on the name of the course. If you need to obtain more information about golfing throughout Trinidad and Tobago can do so reading on Caribbean golf online.

## Sailing and Boating

The following table provides information on firms that can enable you to spend some time out on the open water.

BOATING OPPORTUNITIES ON TRINIDAD

| Name | Phone | Location |
| --- | --- | --- |
| Kelvin Cruise & Travel Service | (868) 659-0271 | Claxton Bay, Central Trinidad |
| T J's Island Cruises | (868) 653-0408 | Trinidad |
| Trinidad Charters | (868) 771-2461 | 6.7 mi. West of Central Port of Spain |

If you want to read about nearby marinas and charter operators, read on Sailing and Boating page.

**Shopping**

You won't want to leave Trinidad and Tobago without picking up a few souvenirs to bring home with you. This can be done at locally owned shops or street markets filled with handmade crafts and wares, or malls similar to those you are probably used to back home. Several places on Trinidad and Tobago allow for duty free shopping, including the Piarco International Airport, West Mall, Long Circular Mall, Excellent City Stores, Maraj and Sons, and Stechers.

If there are some shopping fanatics traveling with you, they'll be interested to know that at least 90 retailers are located in this area. To read our detailed guide to shopping on Trinidad, read on Shopping page.

**Sightseeing**

Yet another great option is experiencing the area's interesting sights. Among other sights, the area has 5 historic sites and various other attractions of interest to visitors Vacationers who enjoy natural surroundings frequently enjoy visiting the area's waterfalls, outdoor parks, and botanical gardens. To visit our complete guide to attractions, read on Attraction page.

Details concerning a firm that will help you enjoy some local sightseeing can be found here:

SIGHTSEEING SERVICES ON TRINIDAD

| Name | Type | Phone | Location |
| --- | --- | --- | --- |
| 2000 Travel | Travel and Tour Operators | (868) 672-2000 | Enterprise, Central Trinidad |
| A Willoughby's Travel Service | Excursions and Sightseeing Service | (868) 652-7747 | San Fernando |
| A'S Travel Service/Thomas Cook Representive | Excursions and Sightseeing Service | (868) 622-7664 | Downtown Port of Spain |
| Carvalho's Agencies | Excursions and Sightseeing Service | (868) 628-0668 | St. James |
| Haygem Tours & Travel Service Ltd | Excursions and Sightseeing Service | (868) 622-4360 | Woodbrook |
| Krystal Tours | Excursions and Sightseeing Service | (868) 674- | Port of Spain |

| | | 5554 | |
|---|---|---|---|
| Latin Tours | Travel and Tour Operators | (868) 662-1847 | 1.6 mi. West of Central St. Augustine |
| Madoo Bird Tours | Nature Tourism Service | (868) 737-2069 | 4.9 mi. Southeast of Central the vicinity of Port of Spain |
| Maria's Tours & Travels Ltd | Excursions and Sightseeing Service | (868) 671-2671 | Chaguanas |
| Naipaul's Tours & Travel Service | Travel and Tour Operators | (868) 623-5516 | Port of Spain |
| Princess Tours | Travel and Tour Operators | (868) 655-8875 | Princes Town, Southern part of Trinidad |
| R & R Transport Tours & Rentals | Travel and Tour Operators | (868) 669-1335 | Trinidad |
| S & R Video & Travel World & Office Depot | Travel and Tour Operators | (868) 667-0351 | Arima, Northern part of Trinidad |
| Shanti's Travel Service | Travel and Tour Operators | (868) 623-0832 | Port of Spain |

## Trinidad

| | | | |
|---|---|---|---|
| Swift Travel Service Ltd | Travel and Tour Operators | (868) 652-2027 | San Fernando |
| Tecu Travel | Travel and Tour Operators | (868) 658-2514 | Gran Couva, Central Trinidad |
| Thomas Cook Representative Travel Service | Travel and Tour Operators | (868) 622-7664 | Port of Spain |
| Trade Winds Travel | Travel and Tour Operators | (868) 623-7531 | Port of Spain |
| Travel Centre Ltd The | Travel and Tour Operators | (868) 622-0112 | Woodbrook |
| Travel House | Travel and Tour Operators | (868) 625-5863 | Port of Spain |
| Travel Network Inc Ltd | Travel and Tour Operators | (868) 623-3651 | Woodbrook |
| Travel Plus Services Ltd | Travel and Tour Operators | (868) 662-0714 | Port of Spain |
| Trevi Tours & Travel | Travel and Tour | (868) | Port of Spain |

| Service | Operators | 622-5536 | |
|---|---|---|---|
| Trinidad & Tobago Sightseeing Tours | Excursions and Sightseeing Service | (868) 628-1051 | St. James |
| Trinidad And Tobago Sight Seeing Tours | Excursions and Sightseeing Service | (868) 628-1051 | The vicinity of Port of Spain |
| Trump Luxury Tours & Executive Coach Services | Excursions and Sightseeing Service | (868) 634-2189 | Chaguaramas, Northwestern part of Trinidad |
| United Travel Service | Travel and Tour Operators | (868) 623-0355 | Port of Spain |
| Winston Nanan-Nanan's Bird Sanctuary Tours | Excursions and Sightseeing Service | (868) 645-1305 | The vicinity of Port of Spain |
| Zion Travels Ltd | Travel and Tour Operators | (868) 674-2375 | Port of Spain |

## Snorkeling

If you like the idea of going snorkeling there's good news -- you'll have plenty of chances to do so off the coast of Trinidad. You can read on

Snorkeling page concerning snorkeling if you'd like to find additional information.

**Spas**

Relaxing in a spa might be one of the most enjoyable parts of your vacation. Spa-goers will find plenty of options, given the fact that there are 13 spas located in this area. To reach our detailed page about spas, read on Spas page.

**Sports**

If you are staying in a resort hotel, chances are they have a lap pool for your enjoyment. They may also have on hand other equipment for water sports, such as jet skiing, snorkeling, and even diving. If your hotel doesn't offer these perks, there are numerous dive shops at which you can purchase or rent equipment and even sign up for lessons and tours.

If you really intend to stay active during your vacation, there are a number of ways for you to do so. Locals certainly don't sit around inactive, as proven by the one gold and three bronze medals won by the country's athletes during the 2012 Summer Olympics.

Hiking groups meet on weekend and holidays to tour natural sites, tennis courts and beach volleyball courts are located on many properties, as are gyms. There are also eight golf courses on Trinidad and Tobago, all in excellent standing.

You can be a spectator as well. Cricket, football, rugby, field hockey, volleyball, and golf are all popular sports to watch on the islands, and chances are one will be in season during your trip.

## Tennis

If you like to play tennis you might want to stay at a hotel that has a tennis court. However, there's only one property where you can play tennis in this area.

## Other Activities

Take a moment to read the following chart to read about other activities.

| OTHER ACTIVITIES ON TRINIDAD | | | |
|---|---|---|---|
| Name | Type | Phone | Location |
| Ato Bolden Stadium | Sporting Event Venue | -- | Green Turtle Cay, Central Trinidad |
| Bio-Fitness Club | Fitness Centers and Instructors | (868) 632-5872 | The vicinity of Port of Spain |
| Caribbean Cinemas (Trincity 8) | Movie Theater | (868) 640- | 3.2 mi. East-Southeast of Central St. |

Trinidad

| | | 8788 | Augustine |
|---|---|---|---|
| Club Monte Carlo Recreational | Recreational Organizations and Clubs | (868) 653-1001 | San Fernando |
| Cox & Sons Barbell Gymn Health & Fitness Centre | Fitness Centers and Instructors | (868) 639-9638 | San Fernando |
| Cyborgs Gym | Fitness Centers and Instructors | (868) 652-9463 | San Fernando |
| Fatima College Sports Grounds | Sporting Event Venue | -- | 1.7 mi. Northwest of Downtown Port of Spain |
| Fitness 2000 Ltd | Fitness Centers and Instructors | (868) 638-7782 | Port of Spain |
| Fitness Center Ltd | Fitness Centers and Instructors | (868) 637-7765 | Downtown Port of Spain |
| Fitness Fanatix Gym | Fitness Centers and Instructors | (868) 675-2321 | Port of Spain |
| Fitness Focus | Fitness Centers and Instructors | (868) 662-2128 | The vicinity of Port of Spain |

| | | | |
|---|---|---|---|
| Funstation | Amusement Arcade | (868) 653-4386 | 1.6 mi. South of Central San Fernando |
| Galactica Family Entertainment Centre | Amusement/Theme Park | (868) 657-5148 | San Fernando |
| Globe Cinema | Movie Theater | (868) 623-1063 | Downtown Port of Spain |
| Gulf View Health & Fitness Centre | Fitness Centers and Instructors | (868) 653-9833 | San Fernando |
| Hasley Crawford Stadium | Sporting Event Venue | -- | 1.7 mi. West-Northwest of Downtown Port of Spain |
| Health Connection | Fitness Centers and Instructors | (868) 636-9066 | Mac Bean, Central Trinidad |
| Himalaya Club | Recreation Center | (868) 638-4023 | Port of Spain |
| Hobosco | Movie Theater | (868) 652-4543 | San Fernando |

## Trinidad

| Name | Type | Phone | Location |
|---|---|---|---|
| Kay Donna Drive In | Movie Theater | -- | 8.7 mi. East of Central Port of Spain |
| Kayak Centre | Jet Ski Rental Service | (868) 633-7871 | Chaguaramas, Northwestern part of Trinidad |
| King's Recreation | Recreation Center | (868) 657-0405 | San Fernando |
| Larry Gomes Stadium | Sporting Event Venue | (868) 643-0437 | 1.5 mi. South of Central Arima |
| Lifestyle Fitness Centre Ltd | Fitness Centers and Instructors | (868) 627-2500 | St. James |
| Little Carib Theatre White & Roberts Sts | Movie Theater | (868) 622-4644 | 1.3 mi. Northwest of Downtown Port of Spain |
| Long Circular Club | Fitness Centers and Instructors | (868) 622-3516 | St. James |
| Massage Therapy Association Of T & T | Massage Therapist | (868) 658-3907 | San Fernando |
| Millenium Fitness Centre | Fitness Centers and Instructors | (868) 671- | Chaguanas |

|  |  | 5906 |  |
|---|---|---|---|
| Muscle Movers Fitness Ltd | Fitness Centers and Instructors | (868) 640-3488 | St. Augustine, Northern part of Trinidad |
| National Cinema | Movie Theater | (868) 652-2343 | 0.2 mi. South-Southeast of Central San Fernando |
| Palladium Cinema | Movie Theater | (868) 662-2775 | 9.5 mi. East of Central Port of Spain |
| Ron's Water Sports | Jet Ski Rental Service | (868) 673-0549 | Chaguanas |
| St Mary's College Tennis Courts | Tennis Club | (868) 628-7066 | St. James |
| The Shape Shop | Fitness Centers and Instructors | (868) 658-5740 | San Fernando |
| Women Only Workout | Fitness Centers and Instructors | (868) 624-5853 | Woodbrook |

If you think that's all, you'll certainly be surprised when you arrive. As you explore Trinidad and Tobago, chances are you'll happen upon more activities that interest you. Do make sure you allow room for a little wiggle in your schedule. Whatever you end up doing, it will be made all the more better because you are in the Caribbean.

# Diving

## Scuba Diving Near Trinidad
**There are dozens of dive sites off the coast of Trinidad and Tobago, and numerous lagoons for snorkeling**

Two of the most popular pastime in the Caribbean are diving; Trinidad and Tobago is no exception. It's hard to resist dipping your head below the surface of the sea and viewing marine life in an area of the world that has such crystal clear visibility and brightly colored tropical fish.

**Diving vs. Snorkeling**

It is important to note the differences between diving and snorkeling before you decide which of the two you would like to try (or if you want to do both activities). Despite the fact that diving and snorkeling can often be done in many of the same areas, they are two very distinct entities.

Scuba (which stands for "self contained underwater breathing apparatus") diving takes the sport a step further. Divers wear an air tank during their underwater journey to allow them to dive deeper and get a closer look at coral reef, marine life, and wreckage sites.

Scuba diving takes a little effort to get started. In Trinidad and Tobago you must be a certified diver in order to rent diving equipment. If you are not certified, you can take instructional courses through local dive shops, and many resorts even offer instructional courses as a perk for staying with them.

You'll find several dive operators and some dive shops to choose from.

**Dive Operators and Shops**

The dive shops you'll be able to find are summarized right below.

| DIVE SHOPS NEAR TRINIDAD | | |
|---|---|---|
| Name | Phone | Location |
| Nick's Water Sports | (868) 743-7334 | Chaguanas |
| Rick's Dive World | (868) 634-3483 | Chaguaramas, Northwestern part of Trinidad |
| Scuba Specialists | (868) 658-3861 | San Fernando |

If you'd like to go diving, you might want to check with DiveTnT. After over 25 years in operation and with over 25,000 dives under their belts, DiveTnT boats an impeccable safety record. In all this time, there have been no drownings or even minor accidents. They are located in Chaguaramas, Trinidad.

Another option is Underwater Works. Unique on the island of Trinidad is Underwater Works, which not only specializes in a full course list of recreational diving, but as a recently certified AWS Educational Institution, they can train up commercial divers as well. If you have interest in training under either type of program, of you're already certified and looking for a great guide team, this is the team for you. You can call them at (868) 743-7334.

A third option is Aquathrills. Specializing in diving and all other manner of outdoor adventure on the island, Aquathrills is your go-to spot when you want to try a little bit of everything. They're found in San Fernando, Trinidad.

Look through the following chart for a list of dive service operators.

DIVE OPERATORS NEAR TRINIDAD

| Name | Phone | Location |
| --- | --- | --- |
| Aquathrills | (868) 290-0304 | San Fernando, Southwestern part of Trinidad |
| Dive Specialists Centre | (868) 634-2919 | Trinidad |
| DiveTnT | (868) 634-2872 | 0.5 mi. East of Central Chaguaramas |
| Underwater Works | (868) 743-7334 | Chaguanas, Central Trinidad |

## Dive Services

Take some time to look through the chart below to get a feel for the approximate cost of typical dive services in this area.

| DIVE SERVICES | | |
|---|---|---|
| Offering Type | Low Rate | High Rate |
| Discover Scuba | $ 85.0 | $ 130.0 |
| Double Tank Dive | $ 85.0 | $ 110.0 |
| Open Water Certification | $ 500.0 | $ 530.0 |
| Single Tank Dive | $ 45.0 | $ 60.0 |

For more information concerning diving, including tips and suggestions for both experienced divers and beginners, check out this detailed guide to diving in the Caribbean online.

## Tips

- ➢ Even with hours of training and a knowledgeable tour guide, there are a few things to keep in mind each time you head out into the water.
- ➢ Pay attention to currents and how your body responds to them; you don't drift too far off course.

- Wear a water proof watch to ensure you don't lose track of time, which can be easy to do underwater.
- Don't feed the fish or touch the animals or coral, this could cause their protective layers to be stripped away.
- Never stand or walk on a reef, and tread carefully in shallow water around reefs. Shuffle your feet to avoid stingrays, and watch out for sea urchin's spines.
- Never wear jewelry. Caribbean fish, barracudas especially, seem to be drawn to shiny objects that look like their natural prey, small silver fish.
- Avoid jellyfish, fire coral, and other stinging creatures.
- Never reach into holes or crevices; animals - especially moray eels - like to make their homes in them.
- Shark sightings are rare, and sharks that are spotted are usually passive. If you do see a shark, stay calm, and if necessary, move slowly out of the water.
- Never remove anything from dive sites and reefs.
- Wear waterproof sunblock. Sunburns are a common side effect of the hot Caribbean sun, even under water.

Planning a day of diving during your Trinidad and Tobago vacation is sure to add a level of excitement to your stay. Whether exploring the numerous coral reef, swimming with the fish, or viewing the spectacular MV Maverick wreckage, the waters of Trinidad and Tobago offer a type of majestic beauty that can't be missed.

# Fishing

## Fishing Near Trinidad
**Charter a boat for fishing, sailing, or both while visiting Trinidad and Tobago**

Fishing has often been overlooked by vacationing anglers, who choose to visit some of the more well known fishing spots in the Caribbean. This is a mistake. The waters off the coast of Trinidad are a great place to drop a line, whether you choose to sail out on a chartered boat or fish at a local beach.

**Fishing**

Depending upon when you travel to Trinidad, the type of fish you can expect to catch varies but you should always expect to catch something. While tuna and shark seem to be available in abundance year-round, other fish are more seasonal. Between June and September African pompano, kingfish, tarpoon, and Spanish mackeral are plentiful; while October through May waters encourage dolphin, wahoo, and sailfish.

If you plan to fish on your Trinidad vacation, there are numerous fishing tours available. These businesses typically supply you with everything you need to fish, including tackle and bait. Some tours even supply food and drink, and have equipment on board for snorkeling. These tours typically cost between $400 and $1000(USD).

You can also take matters into your own hands by renting your own boat and equipment and braving the waters alone. If you choose to go this route, note that the waters off the northwest peninsula of Trinidad and the Gulf of Paria are excellent spots to seek out big game fish. For a more relaxing experience, try fishing off one of the islands' beaches. Las Cuevas Bay and Manzanilla Bay are both great spots.

**Fishing Charters**
If you like the idea of reeling in a big catch during your vacation, there are several charter fishing operators that can take you to the best fishing spots.

If you want to reserve a charter, you might want to check with Island Yacht Fishing Charters. Guests should note that they are welcome to keep up to 30 pounds of all edible fish. After that, the catch remains the property of the boat. They are found in Port of Spain, Trinidad.

A second option is Red Beard Charters. Captain Nicholas Telfer has over 20 years of experience sailing and loves to fish making him the perfect candidate to take you out on your next fishing adventure. Red Beard Charters also cares about the environment, and does its best to leave as little a foot print as possible when out at sea.

Take a look at this table for a listing of local fishing charters.

| FISHING CHARTERS ON TRINIDAD | | |
| --- | --- | --- |
| Name | Phone | Location |
| Island Yacht Fishing Charters | (868) 637-7389 | Port of Spain, Northwestern part of Trinidad |
| Red Beard Charters | -- | Trinidad |
| Trinidad & Tobago Sport Fishing | (868) 634-1717 | Chaguanas, Central Trinidad |

The waters of the Caribbean are unlike any others in the world, so it is only natural that you feel drawn to them on your Trinidad vacation. Give in to the feeling and plan to spend at least a few hours of your vacation aboard a boat reeling in the days catch.

# Golf

Trinidad Golf
**Trinidad comes equipped with five courses**

Golfers traveling to Trinidad and Tobago will be pleasantly surprised that there are several top notch golf courses on the main islands.

Golf courses on Trinidad are open year round, but avid golfers should note that golfing is best done during the dry season, which falls between the months of January and May.

Trinidad and Tobago Golf Association

The Trinidad and Tobago Golf Association (TTGA) works to preserve and promote the game of golf on the islands. All eight golf courses on the island are governed by the TTGA, which means they are held to the highest standards and strive to provide guests with the optimal golfing environment. TTGA hosts several major golf events each year, have programs for youth golfing, and work with the government to promote golf tourism. You can contact the Trinidad and Tobago Golf Association by calling 868-629-7127 or e-mailing ttga@live.com.

## Local Golf Courses

### Brechin Castle Golf Club

Brechin Castle Golf Club: eatures nine holes set amid old sugar plantations. The club house features a restaurant and pool.

### Chaguaramas Golf Club

At the base of Edith Falls sits the nine holes of Chaguaramas Golf Club.

The par-67 course was built on an old bean plantation and plans to expand to an 18 hole course in the coming years. There is also a driving range on property.

## Millennium Lakes Golf & Country Club

Millennium Lakes Golf & Country Club features a driving range, putting greens, and 18 holes. Golfers will also find a pro shop, sports bar, and lounge on property.

## Pointe-a-Pierre Golf Club

Pointe-a-Pierre Golf Club is a par-71 course with 18 holes. The rolling hills make the course a challenging one, especially the back nine.

## St. Andrews Golf Club

St. Andrews Golf Club is an 18 hole course considered to be one of the top in the Caribbean. The course is a hard one, with the first nine holes focusing on distance, and the last nine, accuracy.

## Usine Ste Madeleine Golf Club

Usine Ste Madeleine Golf Club was once referred to as one of the worst golf courses in the Caribbean. Under new management the course has undergone a major transformation in recent years, and now features nine holes on perfectly manicured lawns, and even has a youth program.

## GOLF COURSES

| Name | Phone | Location |
|---|---|---|
| Brechin Castle Golf Club | (868) 636-2311 ext. 5511 | 8.6 mi. (13.8 km) South of Chaguanas |
| Chaguaramas Golf Club | (868) 634-4312 | Airway Road - 7.5 mi. (12.0 km) Northwest of Port of Spain |
| Millennium Lakes Golf & Country Club | (868) 640-8337 | Sunrise Loop Road - 8.0 mi. (12.8 km) Northeast of Chaguanas |
| Pointe-a-Pierre Golf Club | (868) 658-4200 ext. 2403 | 14.1 mi. (22.7 km) South of Chaguanas |
| St. Andrews Golf Club | (868) 629-0066 ext. 26 | Moka, Maraval - 4.5 mi. (7.2 km) Northeast of Port of Spain |
| Usine Ste Madeleine Golf Club | (868) 652-3441 | Manahambre Road - 18.4 mi. (29.6 km) South of Chaguanas |

## Events

There are several golf tournaments held on Trinidad and Tobago each year, or hosted by the TTGA.

## Caribbean Amateur Golf Championship

The Caribbean Amateur Golf Championship is not held on Trinidad and Tobago every year, though it has been the host country several times. At the CAGC, top golfers from participating Caribbean nations

(Bahamas, Barbados, Cayman Islands, Dominican Republic, Jamaica, Puerto Rico, Trinidad and Tobago, Turks and Caicos, and U.S. Virgin Islands) compete for Hoerman Cup.

**Trinidad and Tobago Open Championship**

At the Trinidad and Tobago Open, 120 golfers compete to earn points towards the national title, as well as cash and prizes.

Whether you're a champion golfer or just enjoy hitting a few balls at the driving range, the views at Trinidad and Tobago's courses are worth the trip.

# Nightlife

## Nightlife on Trinidad
**When night falls, Trinidad rises to the occasion**
At one point in recent history, someone who had been to Trinidad and might tell you that Trinidad is the place to go to party, and Tobago is where you hide out and relax. This isn't necessarily the case any longer.

**Bars**

Trinidad and bars have some of the best happy hours around, from two-for-one specials to penny pitchers, and even free samples every now and then. What better time to start your night off than at happy hour? Most of the islands' bars are part of **restaurants**, or at the very least serve bar **food**, so you can get a meal in before beginning your night of debauchery.

**Trinidad Bars:**

- 40/40 Sports Bar and Lounge
- 51° Lounge
- All Out Sports Bar and Grill
- Anchorage
- Aura Cocktail Bar and Restaurant
- Barracuda Bar and Lounge
- The Bay Bar
- The Bight
- Bois Cano
- Cafe Melange
- Carnival Bar
- Checkered Flag Restaurant and Sports Lounge
- Club Senses
- Coco Lounge
- Crobar
- Drink! Wine Bar

- J. Malone's Irish Pub
- Jenny's on the Boulevard
- Lynx Restaurant and Bar
- Mas Camp Pub
- Mangoes Restaurant and Cocktail Lounge
- More Vino
- Paprika Restaurant and Bar
- Rafters
- Sails Restaurant and Bar
- Smokey and Bunty
- Sky Bar and Lounge
- Trotters

## Dance Clubs

Something about being in the Caribbean tends to move people, and make them want to move. If you've got the rhythm in you, head to one of the country's nightclubs instead of a bar to work off some of your extra energy.

## Trinidad Clubs:
- Alchemy
- Hi RPM

- Livin' Room Club
- Pier One
- Space La Nouba
- Sting Night Club
- Tsunami Beach Club
- Zen
- Tobago Clubs:
- Euphoria Lounge
- Kariwak Village

**Other Entertainment**

You don't necessarily have to head into a bar or a club to have good time on Trinidad and Tobago. There are multitudes of other options available. Good wholesome, family fun can be had on a mini-golf course such as Bedrock Mini Golf and Game Center in Port of Spain, dinner theaters, karaoke clubs, and annual events and festivals. Other options include pool halls, live theater, and classical music concerts. If you're interested in seeing a movie during your vacation, there are two movie theaters on Tobago.

ENTERTAINMENT AND NIGHTLIFE

| Name | Type | Phone | Location |
| --- | --- | --- | --- |

| | | | |
|---|---|---|---|
| All Inclusive Bar Services | Bar | (868) 765-3693 | Arima |
| Angie's Place The Pub | Bar | (868) 675-4112 | Port of Spain |
| Bar at Bootleggers | Bar | (868) 6470-8448 | 7.9 mi. Northeast of Chaguanas |
| Baracuda Bar & Lounge | Bar | (868) 634-4000 | Chaguanas |
| Barracuda Bar and Lounge | Bar | (868) 634-4384 | Chaguaramas |
| Caribbean Cinemas (Trincity 8) | Movie Theater | (868) 640-8788 | 8.0 mi. Northeast of Chaguanas |
| Club Monty's Sportsbar | Bar | (868) 653-1966 | San Fernando |
| Columbus Snackette | Bar | (868) 639-8886 | Chaguaramas |
| Daybreak Cafe | Bar | (868) 637-2233 | Trinidad |
| Down Town Beer Garden | Bar | (868) 652-2971 | San Fernando |
| East Lime Recreation Club | Bar | (868) 691-0400 | The vicinity of Port of Spain |
| Globe Cinema | Movie Theater | (868) 623-1063 | Woodbrook |
| Golden Stars Lounge | Lounge | (868) 622-6026 | Port of Spain |
| Greystone Lounge | Lounge | (868) 489-1462 | San Fernando |
| Hobosco | Movie Theater | (868) 652-4543 | San Fernando |
| House of Flava Lounge | Bar | (868) 751-6355 | San Fernando |

# Trinidad

| Name | Type | Phone | Location |
|---|---|---|---|
| Indapa | Bar | (868) 621-5000 | 2.1 mi. East-Northeast of Port of Spain |
| K Mohammed Restaurant & Bar | Bar | (868) 627-5864 | Downtown Port of Spain |
| Kay Donna Drive In | Movie Theater | -- | 7.2 mi. North of Chaguanas |
| Little Carib Theatre White & Roberts Sts | Movie Theater | (868) 622-4644 | Woodbrook |
| Machismo Arcade & Lounge | Lounge | (868) 652-8596 | San Fernando |
| National Cinema | Movie Theater | (868) 652-2343 | 17.8 mi. South of Chaguanas |
| Nice Times Bar | Bar | (868) 659-5233 | The vicinity of Port of Spain |
| Oblivion Entertainment | Bar | (868) 681-4691 | San Fernando |
| Obrien's Beer Garden | Bar | (868) 662-1631 | Valsayn |
| Palladium Cinema | Movie Theater | (868) 662-2775 | St. Augustine |
| Persad Gayandeo | Bar | (868) 668-4839 | Sangre Grande |
| Pier 1 | Bar | (868) 634-4472 | Chaguaramas |
| Rise | Bar | (868) 621-5000 | 2.1 mi. East-Northeast of Port of Spain |

| | | | |
|---|---|---|---|
| Sea View Bar | Bar | (868) 657-8809 | Port of Spain |
| Silver Circle | Bar | (868) 676-0395 | The vicinity of Port of Spain |
| Space La Nouba | Bar | (868) 697-1165 | San Fernando |
| St James Club | Bar | (868) 622-1940 | The vicinity of Port of Spain |
| Sting Nightclub | Night Club | (868) 653-4239 | San Fernando |
| The Bight | Bar | (868) 634-4839 | Chaguaramas |
| V Private Members Club | Bar | (868) 653-2338 | St. James |
| Waterbaby | Bar | (868) 621-5000 | 2.1 mi. East-Northeast of Port of Spain |
| Wheelhouse Pub | Bar | (868) 634-2339 | Chaguanas |
| Yacht Club | Bar | -- | 16.7 mi. South of Chaguanas |
| Zen | Bar | (868) 624-8201 | Port of Spain |

Whether you're looking for something to pass the time at night or you love exploring the nightlife of other countries, you don't want to waste a moment of your time asleep on Trinidad and Tobago.

# Shopping

Shopping on Trinidad

## Shoppers on Trinidad can purchase fine goods from around the globe

Shopping on Trinidad and Tobago is all about variety. In one instant you can be making your way through a busy street bazaar, and the next walking through a department store in the mall. There are also locally owned businesses and various souvenir shops.

## Where to Shop

Outdoor markets are a great place to find the best prices on handicrafts, textiles, produce, and livestock. Charlotte Street in Port of Spain is well known for street vending, but also be on the look out for street vendors on High Street, Main Street in Chaguanas, and the Central Market at Sea Lots.

The bazaar in Port-of-Spain showcases luxury items from around the globe. Shoppers will find everything they could dream of, from Irish linens and English china to Swiss watches and French perfume. At each shop in the bazaar you'll feel as though you've left Trinidad and gone to a whole new country, with the exciting opportunity to bring home a souvenir.

Trinidad's malls come in two forms: arcade and shopping centers. Arcades are what Americans recognize as a shopping mall, with department stores flanking dozens of smaller chains, restaurants, salons, movie theaters, and kiosks. These can be found throughout

Trinidad on Chaguanas, Charlotte, Frederick, Henry, and High Roads. You can expect to pay more at the arcade malls than in the shopping centers.

The shopping centers, meanwhile, are open air shopping plazas, where guests must walk outdoors to move between the shops. In Trinidad, these include City of Grand Bazaar, Cross Crossing Shopping Plaza, Ellerslie Plaza, Falls at West Mall, Gulf City Shopping Complex, Long Circular Mall, MovieTowne Entertainment Complex, Trincity Mall, and Valpark Shopping Centre.

**Gifts and Souvenirs**

Much like the people of Trinidad and Tobago, their craft industry is a vibrant one. If you are looking to take home a souvenir symbolic of the island, look towards the locally made items. In this category you will find mini steel pan drums, leather crafts, beaded jewelry, and wood carvings.

Don't forget about souvenirs you can swallow, from local rum to a wide variety of regional spices.

Also, along with the abundance of products that come from international sources, Trinidad is known for it's great fashion and jewelry industry. Hand printed sarongs and sun dresses, Trinidad t-shirts, painstakingly crafted jewelry, and various other high end designs can be found in boutiques throughout the country.

If you're looking for some souvenirs or gifts you might want to visit Sun Tings, which is found within Port of Spain. Don't return home from Trinidad and Tobago empty handed. Instead, make Sun Tings a planned stop as you tour Port of Spain, where you'll find a huge array of souvenirs to choose from. Visitors will be able to find them at 12 Frederick Street.

Another place to consider is Native Spirit, which is found mi. ( km) to the of Sun Tings. The t-shirts printed by Native Spirit are inspired by the culture of Trinidad and the Caribbean. You'll be able to purchase clothing for kids and adults of all ages and sizes, as well as accessories like caps, beach bags, and more. If you have questions, call them at (868) 622-7969.

A third place to consider is Pocket Pinchers. You can find great deals at Pocket Pinchers every day of the week except for Sunday. Stop by between 8:30 a.m. You can contact them at (868) 653-7413.

Take a look at the following table for information concerning gift and souvenir shops serving this area.

GIFTS AND SOUVENIRS ON TRINIDAD

| Name | Phone | Location |
|---|---|---|
| Carib Collection | (868) 645-5006 | 1.6 mi. West of Central St. Augustine |
| Cocoyea | (868) 628-6546 | St. James, Northern part of Trinidad |
| D Gift Box | (868) 625-9495 | The vicinity of Port of Spain |
| De Lyla's | (868) 662-0770 | 1.6 mi. West of Central St. Augustine |
| Gift City | (868) 665-8179 | Chaguanas |
| Lasercuts | (868) 636-5378 | Mac Bean, Central Trinidad |
| Maharaja Ltd | (868) 662-7252 | 1.6 mi. West of Central St. Augustine |
| Native Spirit | (868) 622-7969 | St. James |
| Paper Mills Ltd | (868) 628-6455 | 3.8 mi. North-Northeast of Central Port of Spain |
| Pocket Pinchers | (868) 653-7413 | San Fernando |
| Pop-In | (868) 622-7262 | 3.8 mi. North-Northeast of Central Port of Spain |
| Ray Cool | (868) 622-7154 | St. James, Northern part of Trinidad |
| Ronald's Jewelery & Gift Shop | (868) 679-0384 | Mac Bean, Central Trinidad |
| Saruna Bajoon | (868) 658-2831 | San Fernando |
| Sheila's Flower & Gift Shop | (868) 653-0020 | San Fernando |

| | | |
|---|---|---|
| Souvenir's Boutique | (868) 653-6255 | San Fernando |
| Stechers Limited | (868) 622-8870 | 1.9 mi. North-Northwest of Downtown Port of Spain |
| Sun Tings | (868) 625-5901 | Port of Spain |
| The Gift Shoppe | (868) 625-2195 | 1.3 mi. Northwest of Downtown Port of Spain |
| The Souvenir Corner | (868) 662-9413 | 1.6 mi. West-Southwest of Central St. Augustine |

## Specialty Shops

One of the more interesting specialty retailers in this area is Horizons Art Gallery. They are found within Trinidad. The vast showroom at Horizons Art Gallery features artwork by a wide berth of popular Trinidadian artists, as well as a few from other Caribbean countries. Collectors and art industry workers will love to tour this spot. Find them at 37 Mucruapo Road.

Another option is Rick's Dive World, which is found mi. ( km) from Horizons Art Gallery. A full-service dive center that offers everything from PADI training and certification to daily dives, this location is also preferred by those who need their dive equipment serviced thanks to the knowledgeable staff that is on-site daily. Visitors can contact them at (868) 634-3483.

The Trinidad Art Society: Once upon a time, a group of artists working in various mediums joined together and decided that Trinidad needed a place that worked to promote modern art amongst the masses. And so the Trinidad Art Society was born. You'll be able to find them on Jamaican Boulevard and St Vincent Circle .

The table directly below lists a few details concerning the specialty shops located on Trinidad.

| SPECIALTY SHOPS ON TRINIDAD | | | |
| --- | --- | --- | --- |
| Name | Type | Phone | Location |
| 101 Art Gallery | Art Gallery | (868) 628-4081 | Woodbrook |
| Anand's Gold & Diamond Collection Ltd | Jewelry Store | (868) 653-1735 | 1.3 mi. South of Central San Fernando |
| Anand's Gold and Diamond Collection | Jewelry Store | (868) 299-3800 | Montrose, Central Trinidad |
| Art Creators | Art Gallery | (868) 624-4369 | Downtown Port of Spain |
| Beach Break Surf Shop | Surfing Gear Store | (868) 632-7873 | Port of Spain, Northwestern part of Trinidad |

## Trinidad

| Name | Type | Phone | Location |
|---|---|---|---|
| Colombian Emeralds Piarco | Jewelry Store | (868) 669-6169 | The vicinity of Port of Spain |
| Dave Jewellers | Jewelry Store | (868) 652-3304 | San Fernando |
| Dipak Jewellers Limited | Jewelry Store | (868) 655-9210 | Princes Town, Southern part of Trinidad |
| Gregory Scott Art Studio | Art Gallery | (868) 717-7545 | Downtown Port of Spain |
| Horizons Art Gallery | Art Gallery | (868) 628-9769 | Trinidad |
| In2 Art Ltd | Art Gallery | -- | St. Ann's |
| Janice's Studio | Jewelry Store | (868) 621-3319 | 1.2 mi. North-Northeast of Central Belmont |
| Jewellery Paradise | Jewelry Store | (868) 657-2229 | 3.1 mi. East-Southeast of Central St. Augustine |
| Kaur Collections | Jewelry Store | (868) 625-9186 | 1.1 mi. Northwest of Downtown Port of Spain |
| Rick's Dive World | Dive Shop | (868) 634-3483 | Chaguaramas, Northwestern part of Trinidad |
| Shiva Jewellers | Jewelry Store | (868) 645-5345 | 1.6 mi. West of Central St. Augustine |
| The Trinidad Art Society | Art Gallery | (868) 622-9827 | Port of Spain |

| Y Art & Framing Gallery | Art Gallery | (868) 628-4165 | Woodbrook |
|---|---|---|---|
| Yasmin's Art and Framing | Art Gallery | (868) 628-4165 | Woodbrook |
| Yolisam Jewellers | Jewelry Store | (868) 633-1131 | Port of Spain, Northwestern part of Trinidad |

## Clothing and Apparel

Enjoy shopping for clothing? Consider dropping by Tish's Fashion -- it's found in Chaguanas. Jeans, tops, dresses, skirts, pants, shoes, hand bags, and perfumes are all for sale at Tish's Fashions. You can style yourself from head to toe, and smell good while doing it when you shop here. The property is situated at 4 Max Street .

A second option is Jungle Glamour -- which is located mi. ( km) from Tish's Fashion. Jungle Glamour sells clothing, sleep wear, lingerie, maternity wear, and bathing suits in loud, expressive prints that make a woman feel almost primal. Additionally, there is a wide selection of handbags and accessories on sale. To contact them, call (868) 652-6958.

Another clothing store is Peter Elias. Having been in the fashion industry for more than three decades, Peter Elias knows a good look when he sees one. That's why you can trust when you walk into his boutique that you will encounter nothing but the best, trendiest designs available. To reach them, call (868) 622-2896.

Lots of the apparel shops located on Trinidad are summarized directly below.

CLOTHING AND APPAREL ON TRINIDAD

| Name | Type | Phone | Location |
| --- | --- | --- | --- |
| Abraham's | Boutique | (868) 672-7646 | Enterprise, Central Trinidad |
| Bang Bang | Boutique | (868) 640-5002 | The vicinity of Port of Spain |
| Candi's | Boutique | (868) 667-8792 | Valencia, Northeastern part of Trinidad |
| Cream Soda | Boutique | (868) 625-7051 | Downtown Port of Spain |
| Flirt By Vs Ltd | Boutique | (868) 627-5458 | 1.3 mi. Northwest of Downtown Port of Spain |
| Geopa Designs | Boutique | (868) 633-6984 | The vicinity of Port of Spain |
| Haven Of Elegance | Clothing Store | (868) 633-4954 | St. James |
| Jabez | Boutique | (868) 662-9954 | 1.6 mi. West of Central St. Augustine |
| Jungle Glamour | Boutique | (868) 652-6958 | San Fernando |
| Livin Trini | Swimwear, Beachwear | (868) 348-9973 | 0.8 mi. Northwest of |

|  | and Sportswear Store |  | Downtown Port of Spain |
|---|---|---|---|
| Nicole's Family Boutique | Boutique | (868) 636-2136 | Downtown Port of Spain |
| Peter Elias | Boutique | (868) 622-2896 | 3.8 mi. North-Northeast of Central Port of Spain |
| Priya's Creations | Boutique | (868) 652-5734 | San Fernando |
| Ray Cool | Sunglasses Shop | (868) 622-7154 | St. James, Northern part of Trinidad |
| Solomon Hadeed & Sons Co Ltd | Boutique | (868) 667-3268 | Arima, Northern part of Trinidad |
| Susan's Exclusive | Boutique | (868) 623-3172 | Port of Spain |
| Tish's Fashion | Boutique | (868) 672-0374 | Chaguanas |
| United Colors Of Benetton | Boutique | (868) 622-8245 | Port of Spain |
| Visions Boutique | Boutique | (868) 645-2668 | 2.2 mi. West-Southwest of Central St. Augustine |
| What's New Pussy Cat | Boutique | (868) 628-0846 | 1.9 mi. North-Northwest of Downtown Port of Spain |

## Food and Grocery

Hungry? Peppercorns is located within Port of Spain, Trinidad. A huge majority of the goods available at Peppercorns are imported from the US, Canada, and Europe, with every items being of gourmet standard. Products include cheeses, meats, frozen foods, desserts, products, dressings, sauces, and a nice selection of gluten free options. To contact them, call (868) 628-5573.

Another place to consider is Bakery Treatz, which is located 12.6 mi. (20.2 km) to the southeast of Peppercorns. Bakery Treatz is open daily from 8:00 a.m. to 7:00 p.m. They're at 75 Rodney Road .

Vanilla Bean Gourmet Store: This shop is open from 9:30 a.m. to 6:00 p.m. You will be able to find them at 145 Munroe Road.

You might want to look through the following chart to learn more.

FOOD AND GROCERY STORES ON TRINIDAD

| Name | Type | Phone | Location |
| --- | --- | --- | --- |
| Bakery Treatz | Bakery | (868) 672-9625 | Chaguanas |
| Chee Mooke Bakery Ltd | Bakery | (868) 623-4607 | Downtown Port of Spain |
| D & S Maharaj Bakery | Bakery | (868) 652-2036 | San Fernando |
| Fernandes Fine | Beer, Wine, and Liquor | (868) 637-1300 | Downtown Port of Spain |

| Wines & Spirits | Store | | |
|---|---|---|---|
| Hi Lo Food Stores | Grocery Store | (868) 627-4456 | Trinidad |
| Maharaj West Side Supermarket Ltd | Grocery Store | (868) 667-6977 | Arima, Northern part of Trinidad |
| Peppercorns | Grocery Store | (868) 628-5573 | 1.9 mi. North-Northwest of Downtown Port of Spain |
| Pricesmart | Grocery Store | -- | 1.6 mi. West of Downtown Port of Spain |
| Puff 'N' Stuff Bakery | Bakery | (868) 657-5920 | San Fernando |
| Puff 'N' Stuff Bakery | Bakery | (868) 657-5920 | San Fernando |
| Ramadhar's Food & Liquor Centre Co Ltd | Beer, Wine, and Liquor Store | (868) 673-0023 | Freeport, Central Trinidad |
| Singh's Liquor Mart | Beer, Wine, and Liquor Store | (868) 628-6252 | St. James |
| Tang Hap Supermarket | Grocery Store | (868) 648-4885 | La Brea, Southwestern part of Trinidad |
| Vanilla Bean Gourmet Store | Grocery Store | (868) 693-0627 | Chaguanas, Central Trinidad |
| Vintage Imports | Beer, Wine, and Liquor | (868) 628-4592 | Woodbrook |

Store

**Duties, Taxes, and Tips**

The official currency of Trinidad and Tobago is the Trinidad and Tobago Dollar (TT$), however, many shops will accept major credit cards and the United States Dollar (USD).

Trinidad does offer guests duty free shopping, allowing $200 worth of gifts, 200 cigarettes, 50 cigars, 1.5 liters of wine or spirits, and perfume to leave the country with visitors at no charge. Visitors will find duty free shopping at Excellent City Stores and Maraj and Sons in Port of Spain, Long Circular Mall in St James, and West Mall in Westmoorings.

The eclectic mix of local products and international goods is what is so special about shopping on Trinidad. Make the most of your $200 duty free limit, and bring home fine goods as well as handcrafted souvenirs.

# Snorkeling

## Snorkeling Around Trinidad

There is some great snorkeling to be found by underwater explorers staying on Trinidad, but the key is knowing where to look.

Unfortunately, snorkeling from most of Trinidad's beaches is not a good idea. Aside from the fact that the waters are not great for visibility, there simply isn't any interesting marine life to be seen. The east coast especially is known for its polluted waters. Instead, your best option will be to charter a boat or sign up for a snorkeling excursion with a local dive or adventure tour operator to visit "down the islands."

"Down the islands" is the term locals use when you take a boat charter out to visit a string of five small islands offshore. These include Five Islands, Diego Islands, Gasparee, Gasparillo, Monos Island, Huevos, and Chacachacare. Boat trips to these islands usually take up a whole day as visitors participate in hikes and birding in addition to snorkeling the reefs that exist here, so plan accordingly. If taking a boat trip is not an option for you and you prefer snorkeling from a beach on mainland Trinidad even if the conditions are not the best, the north coast will be your go-to option. You may also consider doing some island hopping and visit Tobago, where the snorkeling on the Caribbean coast is superb.

Snorkeling Sites

If you want to explore what's below the surface you might enjoy Gaspar Grande Bay. An underwater grotto, this spot offer snorkelers a unique opportunity to snorkel in a cave where they will experience stalactites and stalagmite that form columns of limestone in crystalline waters. This snorkeling site is located on Trinidad.

The chart directly below enables you to get more information about 7 of the best locations to enjoy snorkeling in this area.

SNORKELING SITES NEAR TRINIDAD

| Site | Location |
| --- | --- |
| Balata Bay | 12.4 mi. West of Central Port of Spain |
| Boca de Navios | 14.5 mi. West of Central Port of Spain |
| Bocas del Dragon | 9.9 mi. West of Central Port of Spain |
| Gaspar Grande Bay | 8.1 mi. West of Central Port of Spain |
| The Five Islands | 4.3 mi. West of Central Port of Spain |
| Gasparillo | 7.9 mi. West of Central Port of Spain |
| Maracas Bay | 9.8 mi. Northeast of Central Port of Spain |

## Snorkeling Boat Trips

For some people, the best snorkeling is located off shore.

Information regarding the opportunity to take a boat ride that includes snorkeling are displayed right below.

DAY SAILS AND BOAT TRIPS ON TRINIDAD

| Name | Type | Phone | Location | Island |
|---|---|---|---|---|
| T J's Island Cruises | Boating and Day-Sailing Provider | (868) 653-0408 | Trinidad | Trinidad |

## Snorkeling Services

If you're looking for a place that offers snorkel rentals, excursions, or similar services, you might want to check with DiveTnT. Even after over 25 years of business, this dive center has a perfect record for safety and success. As a bonus, they offer courses on snorkeling safety and rent out top-of-the-line gear. They are located in Chaguaramas, Trinidad.

Take a look at this table to find out more about a firm that offers snorkeling related services.

| SNORKELING SERVICES ON TRINIDAD | | | | |
|---|---|---|---|---|
| Name | Type | Phone | Location | Island |
| DiveTnT | Snorkeling Tour Operator | (868) 634-2872 | 6.7 mi. West of Central Port of Spain | Trinidad |

To learn more about snorkeling, including suggestions and helpful tips for both "old pros" and beginners, check out our detailed discussion of snorkeling in the Caribbean.

Don't let the knowledge of murky waters stamp out your dreams of snorkeling the waters of Trinidad. Instead, make plans for a boat trip to some of the better snorkeling waters offshore and enjoy a full-day adventure of exploration along the way.

## Spas In Trinidad

Spa-goers will find plenty of options, since there are 13 spas in this area.

If you're ready to relax, you might want to check with L'Image Parfaite Day Spa. Offering an oasis of relaxation and rejuvenation, the services featured at L'Image Parfaite Day Spa allow you to stay healthy, feel better, and look younger. They are located in downtown Port of Spain.

Another good option is Jencare Day Spa. Your first stop at Jencare will be to the aromatherapy steam room to detoxify, relax, and prepare your body for other treatments. Next, you'll choose your desired treatment. You can call them at (868) 627-4141.

A third option is Natural Balance - The Natural Medicine Centre. A full service natural medicine center, Natural Balance is actually a retail facility that specializes in high quality natural healing. They also just happen to offer massage therapy as part of their holistic treatment paths. They're located in St. Clair.

Look through the following chart for a few key facts concerning local establishments.

| SPAS ON TRINIDAD | | |
| --- | --- | --- |
| Name | Phone | Location |
| Aveda Day Spa By Tricia | (868) 628-7567 | Woodbrook |
| Better Life Products & Services | (868) 653-0056 | San Fernando |
| De Trini Body Bar | (868) 793-8032 | The vicinity of Port of Spain |
| Gopaul Pearl [L M T] | (868) 658-3907 | San Fernando |
| Indira's Beauty Spa | (868) 655-7580 | Princes Town, Southern part of Trinidad |
| Jackson Isabel | (868) 627-4750 | Downtown Port of Spain |
| Jencare Day Spa | (868) 627-4141 | Woodbrook |
| L'Image Parfaite Day Spa | (868) 720-7474 | Downtown Port of Spain |
| Natural Balance - The Natural Medicine Centre | (868) 628-5649 | St. Clair |
| Shades Beauty Break Salon & | (868) 648-5609 | 1.8 mi. Northeast of Central |

| Spa | | Cap-de-ville |
|---|---|---|
| Swedish Message Institute | (868) 627-3054 | Port of Spain |
| The Exotic Look Beauty Spa | (868) 679-1921 | Gran Couva, Central Trinidad |
| The Sanctuary Day Spa | (868) 625-8040 | 0.5 mi. Northwest of Downtown Port of Spain |

# Attractions on Trinidad

## Discover the splendor of Trinidad

With a large area that consists of lively cities, peaceful suburbs, and quiet country-sides, attractions throughout Trinidad can range greatly. Anyone who is used to other Caribbean island will be pleased that Trinidad is quite different, showing off its South American Proximity in its geography, culture, and history.

**Beaches**

You'll find several beaches to consider on the island. If you prefer having a lot of room around you, you may be pleasantly surprised, some of these beaches are fairly secluded and free from over-development. You can click on each beach name for a detailed review of that specific beach.

Columbus Bay: Located on the Southwestern Peninsula of Trinidad, the bay was named for Christopher Columbus in honor of the fact that he and his crew entered the bay via ship in 1498. Today the beach serves as a semi-popular recreational spot for sun bathing and swimming.

Another alternative that beach-goers can consider is Maracas Bay. Maracas Bay is dazzling with its powder white sands, palm trees, and forestry that encircles the area. The rolling waves are from a water that is blue-green, and are just strong enough on most days for visitors who want to surf.

Mayaro Beach: Mayaro Beach runs parallel to Guayaguayare Mayaro Road. Choose a gravelly side road and make your way east, where you are likely to run into the beach, as it is the longest stretch of beach on the island.

These examples are just a sample of the options worth consideration To get more information on beaches available, read on Beaches page.

## Landmark Attractions

One popular destination is Chaguaramas Military History & Aerospace Museum. It is found on Trinidad. The Chaguaramas Military History and Aviation Museum is located on the former military base, and makes for a great attraction for history and military buffs. The museum was founded by a former member of the Trinidad & Tobago Coastguard.

If you are looking to do more sight-seeing, visit National Museum & Art Gallery. It is located in Port of Spain, Trinidad. The museum offers guests tours of the exhibits where they will guide you through the different areas and describe the importance of each item. You can also feel free to ask them any questions that you might have.

Central Bank Money Museum: Owned and staffed by the Central Bank, this museum will take visitors on a journey across the world and time to see how money, its use, and the way it is made and stored has changed over the years. At this time, the museum is closed for a complete upgrade and renovation, with the expectation that they will reopen in September of 2015.

That's not all -- you'll be able to find other sites to visit. Take advantage of this extended discussion regarding other sites worth visiting on Trinidad if you're looking for additional information.

**Natural Attractions**

Tourists who like the open air are likely to enjoy spending some time at ASA Wright Nature Center. Established in 1967, the ASA Wright Nature Center is a non-profit eco-center dedicated to keeping the protected area in its natural state and study conservation. This spot is particularly favored amongst birders for the 400 birds that nest here annually.

Emperor Valley Zoo is a second attraction that needs mentioning. Although the Emperor Valley Zoo was first built in 1947, it wasn't until 1952 that the doors were opened to the public. To this day it remains a popular family attraction, showcasing both regional and exotic animals and furthering the cause of animal conservation.

Luckily, you'll be able to find a full range choices. To visit our full guide to natural attractions on Trinidad, read on Attraction page.

**Casinos**

Feeling lucky? Visitors interested in trying their luck will find lots of venues where they can do so on the island.

Club Princess Ltd is found in downtown Port of Spain. If the fact that Club Princess Ltd. is the largest casino on Trinidad and Tobago were not enough to draw a crowd, the fact that it is located in the center of Port of Spain and on the busiest street in town would certainly draw a crowd.

Island Club Casino is situated in Valsayn, Trinidad. This 55,000 square foot space features such games as Black Jack, Multi-Action Black Jack, Roulette, Caribbean Stud Poker, and more.

Ma Pau Casino offers a wide array of games for guests to play, including Baccarat, Blackjack, and Poker. Known as one of the best gaming spaces in Port of Spain, Ma Pau Casino offers excellent hospitality to enhance your experience.

Fortunately, you can find plenty of other choices. Read on Casino page dedicated to gaming on Trinidad.

## Beaches on Trinidad

From popular beaches full of amenities to deserted shores, you'll find whatever you want in Trinidad

Although Trinidad isn't known primarily for its beaches, you can still enjoy some sand and surf there. But swimmers should be careful, as riptides and undercurrents abound. Shallow waters can extend quite a distance from shore, so if you don't pay attention, you may suddenly find you've waded too far.

The north coast's calmer waters and natural beauty make its beaches the best for swimming on Trinidad. Changing rooms, bathrooms, and food are available at some of the beaches in this area. Here you'll find Maracas Bay, the most popular beach among locals and tourists alike. But if you want to get away from the crowds, you can find more tranquil places, as well.

Near Port of Spain on the northwest coast, locals frequent several beaches offering swimming, surfing, and kayak rentals. However, you won't find the same picturesque quality here as you will on the north coast. And you may find the waters to be polluted, which could make swimming less appealing.

The island's northeast coast, with its rocky shores and dangerous waters, is best for surfing. Prime surfing season here runs from November to April. Swimming isn't recommended, but if you absolutely must try it, talk to the locals to find the safest spots.

If you yearn for long stretches of unspoiled coastline, take a drive down the east coast. Aside from a few small towns dotting the countryside, you'll find little else here but sand and palm trees. Waters here tend to look muddy, and watch out for those undertows. Trinidad's beaches are a fun supplement to your main activities. But if you plan on making beach excursions the cornerstone of your trip, Tobago offers much more.

## The Area's Beaches

There are a large number of beaches to consider on the island. If you're looking for a quiet getaway, you will be pleased to know that several of the beaches are fairly secluded and quiet. Simply click on the name of the beach to get additional information about that part of the coast.

Mayaro Beach: Lined by lush trees in most places along the beach, the sand here ranges from a light to dark tan, getting darker the closer it gets to the sea. The water can be rough and is known for rip currents so much so that lifeguards are almost always present during daylight hours.

Another alternative that beach-goers can consider is Cedros Bay. Cedros Bay is set on the Southwestern Peninsula, and can be accessed off of the Southern Main Road.

Guayaguayare Bay Beach: On the southeast tip of Trinidad lies Guayaguayare Bay Beach. This beach is not necessarily popular for swimming and sun bathing, but rather for fishing and sightseeing.

The beaches on Trinidad are displayed in the following chart.

BEACHES ON TRINIDAD

| Name | Location | Coast |
| --- | --- | --- |
| Balandra Bay | 0.4 mi. South of Central Rampanalgas | North East |
| Blanchisseuse Beach | 0.7 mi. East-Northeast of Central Blanchisseuse | North |
| Cedros Bay | 1.5 mi. West of Central Bonasse | South West |

| Columbus Bay | 2.4 mi. West-Southwest of Central Fullarton | South West |
| --- | --- | --- |
| Cyril Bay | 1.0 mi. West of Central Maracas Bay | North |
| Grande Riviere Bay | 0.1 mi. Northeast of Central Grande Riviere | North East |
| Granville Beach | 0.6 mi. North-Northwest of Central Granville | South West |
| Guayaguayare Bay Beach | 0.9 mi. West of Central Settlement | South East |
| Irois Bay Beach | 2.3 mi. West-Southwest of Central Point Fortin | South West |
| Las Cuevas Bay | 3.3 mi. East-Northeast of Central Maracas Bay | North |
| Macqueripe Bay | 4.2 mi. North-Northeast of Central Chaguaramas | North West |
| Manzanilla Beach | 1.5 mi. East of Central Lower Manzanilla | East |
| Maracas Bay | 0.1 mi. East-Southeast of Central Maracas Bay | North |
| Matura Bay | 4.4 mi. East of Central Oropouche | North East |
| Mayaro Beach | 0.9 mi. South of Central St. Margaret | South East |
| Quinam Beach | 4.8 mi. South of Central Siparia | South |
| Salibea Bay | 1.9 mi. East of Central Old Road Town | North East |
| Saline Bay | 0.4 mi. Northeast of Central Salybia | North East |
| Scotland Bay | 2.3 mi. Northwest of Central Chaguaramas | North West |
| Tyrico Bay | 1.2 mi. East of Central Maracas Bay | North |

Bear in mind, Trinidad has other attractions. To reach our page about other attractions, read on Attraction page.

# Casinos

## Trinidad Casinos

**There are more than a dozen casinos to choose from on Trinidad**

Those who yearn for glitz, glamor, and high stakes on their Trinidad vacation don't have to wish they'd vacationed in Las Vegas instead. Trinidad is home to numerous casinos, where tourists can try their luck while playing one of many games of chance.

**Where to Find Gambling**

Ready for some action? Vacationers interested in testing their luck in some gaming action will discover plenty of places to go. Click on the name to learn more.

Ma Pau Casino is found within Woodbrook, Trinidad. Known as one of the best gaming spaces in Port of Spain, Ma Pau Casino offers excellent hospitality to enhance your experience.

Take a minute to read the following table for more information about gaming venues.

GAMBLING ON TRINIDAD

| Name | Type | Phone | Location |
|---|---|---|---|
| Bob's Racing Service | Gambling Site | (868) 622-2066 | Port of Spain |
| Club Casablanca | Casino | (868) 645-8733 | 1.5 mi. East of Central Belmont |
| Club Casanovas | Gambling Arcade | (868) 662-1253 | 1.0 mi. East of Central St. Augustine |
| Club De Vegas | Gambling Site | (868) 623-1118 | Downtown Port of Spain |
| Club Monte Carlo | Casino | (868) 653-1001 | San Fernando, Southern part of Trinidad |
| Club Phoenix | Gambling Site | (868) 664-0463 | Central Trinidad |
| Club Play 2 Win | Casino | -- | Downtown Port of Spain |
| Club Princess Ltd | Gambling Site | (868) 625-5723 | Downtown Port of Spain |
| Club Regal | Gambling Site | (868) 652-8100 | San Fernando, Southwestern part of Trinidad |
| Club Solitaire | Gambling Site | (868) 662-8000 | 1.6 mi. West-Southwest of Central St. Augustine |
| Diamond Members Club | Gambling Site | (868) 622-7563 | Woodbrook |
| Fair Chance Racing | Gambling Site | (868) 624- | Downtown Port of Spain |

# Trinidad

| | | | |
|---|---|---|---|
| Service | | 2387 | |
| Federal Racing Service | Gambling Site | (868) 665-4992 | Chaguanas |
| Flamingo Private Members Club | Gambling Site | -- | Princes Town, Southern part of Trinidad |
| Golden Tulip Kapok Casino | Casino | (868) 622-9677 | 1.7 mi. North-Northwest of Downtown Port of Spain |
| Goldgate Casino and Pub | Casino | (868) 624-8249 | Downtown Port of Spain |
| Goodwood Racing Service | Gambling Site | (868) 645-7340 | The vicinity of Port of Spain |
| Island Club Casino | Casino | (868) 645-3333 | 1.6 mi. West of Central St. Augustine |
| La Bonne Vie Casino | Casino | (868) 657-9278 | San Fernando, Southern part of Trinidad |
| Ma Pau Casino | Casino | (868) 627-6214 | 1.4 mi. Northwest of Downtown Port of Spain |
| New Market Racing Service | Gambling Site | (868) 622-1114 | St. James |
| Sam's Racing Service | Gambling Site | (868) 663-2138 | Chaguanas |
| Sands Casino | Casino | (868) 653-7465 | San Fernando, Southwestern part of Trinidad |

| Track Investors | Gambling Site | (868) 657-5451 | San Fernando |
| White Diamond Casino | Casino | (868) 636-7365 | Gran Couva, Central Trinidad |
| Winners Club | Gambling Site | (868) 628-6333 | Woodbrook |

Of course, Trinidad has additional attractions. To reach our full guide to other attractions, read on Attraction page.

# Trinidad Landmarks

## There is more to Trinidad than the beaches

The island of Trinidad abounds with fascinating sites that should be on your list of "Things To See." Between the unique architecture and the historical significance of the top landmarks, each spot proves to offer something of interest

### Museums

Assuming you like to expand your knowledge of other places and cultures, you should consider visiting a museum during your time on Trinidad. Just click on each place's name to see detailed information.

A common landmark for vacationers is Chaguaramas Military History & Aerospace Museum. It is found within Trinidad. The Chaguaramas

Military History and Aviation Museum is located on the former military base, and makes for a great attraction for history and military buffs. The museum was founded by a former member of the Trinidad & Tobago Coastguard.

Another common landmark for vacationers is Central Bank Money Museum. It is found within downtown Port of Spain. The Money Museum has three main rooms that will take visitors through three different topics. The first room deals with money in general, and how it has evolved around the world from simple stones to gold, and today to paper currency, debit and credit cards, and completely electronic currency.

National Museum & Art Gallery: The museum offers guests tours of the exhibits where they will guide you through the different areas and describe the importance of each item. You can also feel free to ask them any questions that you might have.

The table below lists a few details concerning some museums you might enjoy on the island.

MUSEUMS ON TRINIDAD

| Name | Phone | Location | Island |
|---|---|---|---|
| Angostura Museum and | (868) 623- | 2.4 mi. East of Central | Trinidad |

| Barcant Butterfly Collection | 1841 ext. 255 | downtown Port of Spain | |
| --- | --- | --- | --- |
| Central Bank Money Museum | (868) 625-2601 ext. 2151 | Downtown Port of Spain | Trinidad |
| Chaguaramas Military History & Aerospace Museum | (868) 634-4391 | 5.6 mi. West-Northwest of Central Port of Spain | Trinidad |
| Indian Caribbean Museum of Trinidad and Tobago | (868) 673-7007 | Trinidad and Tobago | None |
| National Museum & Art Gallery | (868) 623-5941 | 0.7 mi. North of Downtown Port of Spain | Trinidad |

## Historical Sites

Enjoy discovering the history of places you visit? If so, you should consider visiting one or two of these historical attractions during your vacation.

A common landmark for vacationers is President's House. It is found in St. Ann's, Trinidad. While the President's House serves as the private residence of the president of Trindad and Tobago, it also has an official capacity as well. From the neighboring Botanical Gardens, visitors can view the house whenever they choose.

An alternative landmark could be Fort Picton. It's a historical site Built by the British in 1797 fearing an imminent invasion by France or Spain,

Fort Picton was the solution. The island's governor hoped that this single fort would be enough to hold off the other European empires.

Stollmeyer's Castle: Known as one of the "Magnificent Nine" historic buildings in Queen's Park West, this property is a historic home that was built to model a castle in Scotland. It's architecture is certainly impressive, and although it has had many uses over the years, today it is a popular attraction for tourists to visit.

Be sure to look at the table just below to learn more about historic sites on Trinidad.

HISTORIC SITES ON TRINIDAD

| Name | Phone | Location |
| --- | --- | --- |
| Fort George | (868) 639-3970 | 2.1 mi. North of Central Port of Spain |
| Fort Picton | -- | 1.0 mi. East of Downtown Port of Spain |
| Hayes Court | -- | Downtown Port of Spain |
| President's House | (868) 624-1261 | 1.6 mi. North of Downtown Port of Spain |
| Stollmeyer's Castle | -- | 1.5 mi. North-Northwest of Downtown Port of Spain |

## Miscellaneous Landmarks

Visitors may discover some other interesting places worth visiting on the island.

Other kinds of landmarks on the island are provided here:

| MISCELLANEOUS LANDMARKS ON TRINIDAD | | |
|---|---|---|
| Name | Type | Location |
| Brian Lara Promenade | Tourist Attraction | Downtown Port of Spain |
| Brigand Hill Lighthouse | Lighthouse | 0.7 mi. South of Central Lower Manzanilla |
| Brighton Range Front | Lighthouse | 0.6 mi. North of Central La Brea |
| Chacachacare Island | Lighthouse | 15.0 mi. West of Central Port of Spain |
| Espalon Point | Lighthouse | 2.1 mi. South West of Central Chaguaramas |
| St. Vincent Jetty Range Rear | Lighthouse | Downtown Port of Spain |

Bear in mind, Trinidad has other attraction types. To find out about other other attractions for Trinidad, read on Attraction page.

Religious Sites

Located in Independence Square in Port of Spain, the Cathedral of the Immaculate Conception was built in the 1820s, and is well visited because of its architecture. The cathedral still holds daily services, and visitors are welcome to attend.

Artisans from India constructed the Dattatreya Yoga Centre on Trinidad, complete with an 85-foot statue of the god Hanuman. The temple is an active place of worship, so no pictures may be taken inside, but guests are welcome to snap photos on the grounds outside.

Despite being destroyed in a fire, today the Holy Trinity Cathedral in Port of Spain looks very much like it did when it was built in the 1820s. Visitors are welcome to enter the cathedral and sit in on a daily service.

The Presbyterian church in Port of Spain is Greyfriars Church. It was built in the 19th century, and is a simple, but beautiful structure.

Whether you are on a spiritual journey and hope to attend services at some of the islands' historical religious spots, enjoy learning about military history, or can't resist a trip to the top of a lighthouse for a look out over the surrounding areas, Trinidad and Tobago has something to offer you. Leave at least one day of your trip open for site-seeing, and you're sure to return home with a few stories to tell.

# Natural Attractions

## Natural Attractions on Trinidad
**Trinidad is a popular bird watching destination**
With a total area of 1,981 square miles, the topography of Trinidad and Tobago is diverse. From mangrove swamps to mountain tops, vacationers on a mission to get outdoors have the opportunity to explore it all.

**Nature Preserves and Hiking**
Do you hope to enjoy more of your vacation seeing the local flaura and fauna? You might be happy to find out that the island has a good selection of nature preserves on it.

ASA Wright Nature Centeris a nature preserve northern Trinidad. With birding of special interest to most visitors at ASA Wright Nature Center, the center has created the Dunston Cave especially for the breeding of the nocturnal Oilbird. There are over 400 birds that nest throughout the property, as well as 97 mammals, 55 reptiles, 617 butterflies, 25 amphibians, and over 2,200 types of plants.

Vacationers wanting to locate a another great natural attraction should consider visiting choices like Caroni Bird Sanctuary. Daily boating trips and other tours are available daily. These include a

General Tour which takes place at 4:00 p.m., a Photography Tour, a Bird Watching Tour, a Family Picnic Tour, and a Fishing Tour.

Pointe-a-Pierre Wildfowl Trust: Pointe-à-Pierre Wild Fowl Trust teaches daily environment education programs about local waterfowl and their link to all human beings, as well as the wetland ecosystems, with the end result being a tour of the property.

Take a look at the table just below for more information about your options.

NATURE PRESERVES AND HIKING ON TRINIDAD

| Name | Type | Location |
| --- | --- | --- |
| ASA Wright Nature Center | Nature Sanctuary/Wildlife Reserve | 5.6 mi. North of Central Arima |
| Arena Forest Reserve | Nature Sanctuary/Wildlife Reserve | 5.7 mi. Southeast of Central Arima |
| Blanchisseuses Forest Reserve | Nature Sanctuary/Wildlife Reserve | 2.8 mi. Southeast of Central Blanchisseuse |
| Caroni Bird Sanctuary | Nature Sanctuary/Wildlife Reserve | 5.8 mi. Southeast of Central downtown Port of Spain |

| Caroni Lagoon National Park | Nature Sanctuary/Wildlife Reserve | 5.6 mi. Southeast of Central downtown Port of Spain |
|---|---|---|
| Central Range Forest Reserve | Nature Sanctuary/Wildlife Reserve | Central Trinidad |
| Forest & Nature Reserve | Nature Sanctuary/Wildlife Reserve | 2.9 mi. East-Southeast of Central Maracas Bay |
| Matura Forest Reserve | Nature Sanctuary/Wildlife Reserve | 4.0 mi. Northwest of Central Matura |
| Melajo Forest Reserve | Nature Sanctuary/Wildlife Reserve | 1.9 mi. North of Central Oropouche |
| Parva Forest Reserve | Nature Sanctuary/Wildlife Reserve | 5.8 mi. East of Central Blanchisseuse |
| Pointe-a-Pierre Wildfowl Trust | Nature Sanctuary/Wildlife Reserve | Central Trinidad |
| Siparia Reserve | Nature Sanctuary/Wildlife Reserve | 0.8 mi. Northeast of Central Siparia |
| Southern Watershed | Nature | 2.4 mi. South West of Central |

Trinidad

| Forest Reserve | Sanctuary/Wildlife Reserve | Morne Diablo |
|---|---|---|
| St. David Forest Reserve | Nature Sanctuary/Wildlife Reserve | 2.7 mi. South of Central Grande Riviere |
| Trinity Hills Wildlife Sanctuary & Reserve | Nature Sanctuary/Wildlife Reserve | 5.7 mi. West of Central Guayaguayare |
| Tumpuna Forest Reserve | Nature Sanctuary/Wildlife Reserve | 1.9 mi. North of Central Four Roads |
| Victoria Mayoro Forest Reserve | Nature Sanctuary/Wildlife Reserve | 6.5 mi. South of Central Ecclesville |
| Yarra Forest Reserve | Nature Sanctuary/Wildlife Reserve | 1.5 mi. South-Southwest of Central Blanchisseuse |

## Waterfalls

Even though most vacationers are attracted by the beaches, that isn't the only way to enjoy the natural wonders available. Trinidad offers some great options, including two waterfalls.

You should consider visiting Edith Falls, which is northwestern Trinidad. A sign pointing to Edith Falls will guide you to the start of your hike just before the Chaguaramas Golf Course.

The following table summarizes more details regarding waterfalls.

| WATERFALLS ON TRINIDAD | | |
|---|---|---|
| Name | Type | Location |
| Edith Falls | Waterfall | 3.4 mi. North of Central Chaguaramas |
| Maracas Waterfall | Waterfall | 6.6 mi. Northeast of Central Belmont |

## Parks and Botanical Gardens

Visitors can visit one of the many parks, as well as 2 botanical gardens on Trinidad.

To surround yourself with beautiful tropical vegetation, consider visiting Royal Botanical Gardens, which is located in St. Ann's, Trinidad. One of the oldest gardens in the world, the Royal Botanical Gardens was established in the year 1818, and for almost two centuries have been pleasing visitors with the colorful flowers and native plants.

The parks and gardens worth looking into are provided below.

| PARKS AND GARDENS ON TRINIDAD |
|---|

# Trinidad

| Name | Type | Location |
|---|---|---|
| Jackson Square | Park | 1.5 mi. North-Northwest of Downtown Port of Spain |
| Lord Harris Square | Park | 0.6 mi. North of Downtown Port of Spain |
| Memorial Park | Park | 0.8 mi. North of Downtown Port of Spain |
| Nelson Mandela Park | Park | 1.5 mi. Northwest of Downtown Port of Spain |
| Public Service Association Grounds | Park | Downtown Port of Spain |
| Queen's Park Oval | Park | 1.4 mi. Northwest of Downtown Port of Spain |
| Queen's Park Savannah | Park | Downtown Port of Spain |
| Queen's Royal College Sports Ground | Park | 1.3 mi. Northwest of Downtown Port of Spain |
| Rock Garden | Botanical Garden | 1.5 mi. North-Northwest of Downtown Port of Spain |
| Royal Botanical Gardens | Botanical Garden | 1.6 mi. North of Downtown Port of Spain |
| Siegert Square | Park | 1.3 mi. Northwest of Downtown Port of Spain |
| Victoria Square | Park | Downtown Port of Spain |
| Wild Flower Park | Park | 1.6 mi. North-Northwest of Downtown |

|  |  | Port of Spain |
|---|---|---|
| Woodford Square | Park | Downtown Port of Spain |

## Zoos and Aquariums

If the thought of passing some time with interesting animals tickles your fancy, you should visit Emperor Valley Zoo. Although the Emperor Valley Zoo was first built in 1947, it wasn't until 1952 that the doors were opened to the public. To this day it remains a popular family attraction, showcasing both regional and exotic animals and furthering the cause of animal conservation.

| ZOOS ON TRINIDAD | | | |
|---|---|---|---|
| Name | Type | Location | Island/th> |
| Emperor Valley Zoo | Zoo | 1.6 mi. North of Downtown Port of Spain | Trinidad |

## Land Formations

Another idea is to visit some of the more interesting area land formations. Other options like these on Trinidad are shown in the chart below.

| LAND FORMATIONS ON TRINIDAD |
|---|

## Trinidad

| Name | Type | Location |
|---|---|---|
| Balata Bay | Bay | 9.3 mi. Northeast of Central Port of Spain |
| Blanchisseuse Bay | Bay | 1.0 mi. East-Northeast of Central Blanchisseuse |
| Boca de Navios | Bay | Northwestern part of Trinidad |
| Bocas del Dragon | Bay | Northwestern part of Trinidad |
| Carenage Bay | Bay | 1.5 mi. East of Central Chaguaramas |
| Columbus Bay | Bay | 2.4 mi. West-Southwest of Central Fullarton |
| Cyril's Bay | Bay | 3.0 mi. West of Central Maracas Bay |
| Gaspar Grande Bay | Bay | 8.1 mi. West of Central Port of Spain |
| Grand Riviere Bay | Bay | 0.5 mi. North of Central Grande Riviere |
| Las Cuevas Bay | Bay | 3.3 mi. Northeast of Central Maracas Bay |
| Madamas Bay | Bay | 3.6 mi. West of Central Sandy Point |
| Maracas Bay | Bay | 0.7 mi. East-Northeast of Central Maracas Bay |
| Matelot Bay | Bay | 0.4 mi. North-Northeast of Central Sandy Point |
| Matura Bay | Bay | 1.9 mi. East of Central Matura |
| Mayaro Bay | Bay | 1.2 mi. Southeast of Central St. Margaret |
| Paria Bay | Bay | 5.3 mi. East of Central Blanchisseuse |
| Pitch Lake | Lake | 0.8 mi. South West of Central La Brea |
| Salybia Bay | Bay | 0.6 mi. Northeast of Central Old Road Town |

| Tyrico Bay | Bay | 1.8 mi. Northeast of Central Maracas Bay |
| Yarra Bay | Bay | 1.3 mi. Northwest of Central Blanchisseuse |

For more nature on Trinidad and Tobago, just walk outside and take a look around. The beauty of Mother Nature's bounty abounds no matter where you look.

# Cruising to Trinidad

Cruise travel lets travelers see more than one island in the Caribbean

Cruises are a great way to see as many Caribbean islands as possible in one vacation. You may not stay long at each port, but cruises can ensure you enjoy the voyage as much as the destinations. Relaxing in style while taking in the ship's activities, amenities, and the blue waters of the Caribbean is how many people choose to enjoy a vacation.

Trinidad and Tobago's southern location - the islands are just seven miles from Venezuela - means cruise ships do not stop there as frequently as other ports in the Caribbean. However, the number of cruise travelers to the islands has been increasing in the past 15 years, and in the second half of the 1990s, the number of cruise ships visiting the islands nearly doubled.

Several cruise line companies offer excursions that stop in one of the two cruise ports on the islands. Passengers to Trinidad will stop at Port of Spain, while passengers to Tobago will stop at Scarborough. The Port Authority can be contacted at 868-624-9734. Also try 868-625-3055 on Trinidad or 868-639-2181 on Tobago. The port in Port of Spain offers transportation, shopping, and communications services for disembarking cruise ship passengers.

## Cruise Lines

| Cruise Line | Contact Information |
| --- | --- |
| Fred Olsen Cruises | 0-14-73-74-61-75<br>http://www.fredolsencruises.com/ |
| Holland America | 1-877-SAIL-HAL<br>http://www.hollandamerica.com |
| Ocean-Village Cruises | 0-845-358-5000<br>http://www.oceanvillageholidays.co.uk/ |
| Peter Deilmann Cruises (Deutschland) | 800-348-8287<br>http://www.deilmann-cruises.com/ |
| Princess Cruises | 800-PRINCESS<br>http://www.princess.com |

| Saga Cruises | 0-800-096-0083 |
| --- | --- |
| | http://www.saga.co.uk |
| Seabourn Cruises | 800-929-9391 |
| | http://www.seabourn.com |
| Windjammer | 800-327-2601 |
| | http://www.windjammer.com |
| Windstar Cruises | 800-258-7245 |
| | http://www.windstarcruises.com |

## Ships

Ships from different cruise lines vary in size and passenger capacity. Often, the more luxurious cruises are held aboard smaller ships, with an army of staff members serving only a few hundred passengers. Larger cruise ships, whose size can help prevent seasickness, can hold thousands of passengers.

When considering the size of the boat, think about how much personal space you require to be comfortable. A smaller ship with few passengers may offer more space per passenger than a larger ship with many passengers. Another factor to consider is the number of wait and service staff members on the boat compared to the number of passengers on board. If the ratio of waitstaff to passengers is low, the level of customer service aboard the vessel should generally be high.

**Classes, Types, and Cost**

In addition to considering the size of the ship, vacationers should consider the class, type, and cost of their cruise travel when preparing to book spots on the ship.

Some cruise lines and companies offer specialty cruises that are aimed at catering to a specific type of customer. Specialty cruises often host gays and lesbians, singles, families, or senior citizens.

Cruise class can also help determine the cruise ship and itinerary package appropriate to your needs. Typical cruises offer an extensive list of amenities and benefits to their guests including childcare, fitness centers, pools, restaurants, clubs, and entertainment programs such as music and theater. Higher classes of cruise travel may include extra amenities and also include a higher level of service, a higher quality of products, and more space. Passengers who are looking for a high level of customer service and amenities should consider the upgrade to the higher cruise classes.

Fares on all cruise classes vary depending on the season (high or off) and travel plans, so travelers who are more flexible will have better options for finding deals. Items such as drinks and gratuities are not generally included in the cost of your fare. Soft drinks and alcohol can prove to be a significant part of your budget. Also, the costs of your trip when you are not on the boat are not covered, so travelers should have a budget for shopping, eating, and recreational activities on the islands.

**When and Where**

The cruise season for the Caribbean follows the high season for general travel to the Caribbean. Popular travel times range from mid December to April, while off-season travel times coincide with rain and hurricane seasons in the Atlantic, from May to the end of November. Although hurricane season should certainly be an important consideration for travelers, cruises are generally offered year-round by major companies, and fares may be reduced for travel during the off season.

Due to its southeastern location in the Caribbean, not all cruise ships regularly call at Trinidad and Tobago. The cruise itineraries that do may be longer cruise periods, such as 10 or 12 days. Cruise ship passengers will generally only spend eight or nine hours on each island that they visit before moving on to their next destination.

**Cabins and Packing**

The location of your room can affect your cruise experience, and travelers should be mindful of several factors, such as children and noise, when requesting the location of their room.

Cabin requests are divided into run-of-the-ship cabins and perfect cabins. Those who request run-of-the-ship cabins may choose between an inner or outer cabin. The booking of the cabin floor and type will not be final until the departure date nears, so travelers will not know whether they have received their request until that time. Perfect cabins come at an increased cost but allow travelers the luxury of choosing the type of cabin and the type of room they wish to have. This may be a good option if you need a certain type of cabin. Those who are prone to seasickness, for example, should request an inner cabin, which won't rock as much as an outer cabin. Others who wish to have an ocean-view room should be sure to specify an outer room with an ocean view, as not all outer rooms have them.

Noise should be another consideration when choosing your room. Rooms that are next to high public-traffic areas, including stairwells or gyms, or rooms that are next to facilities such as restaurants or bars are likely to be noisier during the night than cabins that are farther from these areas. Travelers who are concerned about noise and sleep should make attempts to secure rooms away from these areas.

Travelers with children should also consider which type of room is appropriate - some feel rooms with balconies are not safe for children.

Packing is a final important consideration when traveling. Cruise ship travelers must pack efficiently because space is very limited. Pack clothes that are suitable for the ship as well as the various destinations. Also bring beach and activewear, including swimsuits, hats, sunglasses, sandals, and tank tops. On many islands, wearing swimsuits or shorts in restaurants or while shopping is considered inappropriate, so travelers should also be sure to pack casual trousers and shirts to look presentable on the islands. Depending on the cruise type and class, some of the ship's restaurants and activities may require dress from casual to formal, so travelers should check ship policies before packing to see whether ties, jackets, and more formal dresses will be required.

For travelers who want to experience Trinidad and Tobago along with several other islands in the Caribbean, cruise lines can be a stylish and relaxing way to go.

## Food on Trinidad

Travelers have many options for dining on Trinidad and Tobago

Many dining options are available on Trinidad and Tobago, with international cuisine providing the inspiration for many of the islands' most popular local delicacies.

**Restaurants**

Some enjoy the quick comfort of popular street vendors and bake stands that serve hot and delicious sandwiches and rotis. These rotis and shark bake stands provide quick but delicious, and certainly very quintessential Trinidad and Tobago culinary styles. International and local fast food chains are also available on the islands for quick and affordable meals, including pizza, chicken, and Chinese food. Meals at chains and bake or rotis vendors generally costs less than $10(USD) and can go as low as $3(USD).

Some restaurants allow travelers to enjoy inventive world and local cuisine, serving Spanish, French, Indian, and Chinese-influenced dishes, while American and native Caribbean specialties are also usually featured on most menus. More upscale restaurants serve European and Caribbean cuisine for approximately $30(USD) per person, with soup, starter, main course, and dessert. Many restaurants on the islands feature menus that reflect an array of cultural influences, as well as a wide range of prices. Moderately priced restaurants allow guests to eat for as little as $10(USD) and can also serve dishes that exceed $30(USD). These price ranges allow travelers on all budgets to sample fare in the islands' many unique establishments.

Travelers should be aware that restaurants on the island are mainly concentrated in tourist areas. Ariapita Avenue in Port-of-Spain in particular is known as "restaurant strip," but Queen's Park Savannah, St. Clair, and Woodbrook also have their share of worth-while restaurants. Finding restaurants can become very difficult when traveling to the underdeveloped areas, but these are also the best locations in which to find the most authentic island fare.

Additionally, many of Trinidad and Tobago's restaurants are located along the coast in old colonial buildings that have been adapted into eateries. These locations are largely unpretentious, and guests needn't feel as though they need to dress to the nines to sit down for a meal. While bathing suits should be kept to the beaches, a pair of slacks and t-shirt won't get you thrown out of the facility.

More and more recently, hotels have been providing the main dining setting for island guests. This is especially true at All-inclusive resorts, where meals are included in the price of the room. Depending upon the resort and the restaurant, this food could range from comfort foods from your hometown to culinary masterpieces with international flavor. Still, adventurous vacationers who are looking forward to sampling local foods may find it best to venture off property, at least for a few meals. If you are still undecided where to stay, you can learn about restaurants at specific hotels in several ways. First, consider visiting our article listing the Best Hotels for Dining Options. Or, select hotels that interest you from our extensive list (A to Z: Hotels in Detail), and read about their restaurants, as well as other nearby dining options within our detailed discussion of each property.

## Culinary Styles
### Food
The foodstuff of Trinidad and Tobago are heavily influenced by the islands' immigrant population. Local dishes take bits and pieces from Indian, Chinese, Latin, Creole, and even Eurpoean cultures. The spicier the better is often the motto with food items such as curry, though many vacationers might see dishes like armadillo and opposum stew and think the more adventurous the better is the real motto of Trinidad and Tobago. It's true that the food on Trinidad and Tobago is probably unlike anything you've tried back in your home town. You can avoid being surprised by unique flavors by learning about island eats at our page dedicated to educating visitors on popular Trinidad and Tobago foods: Culinary Styles on Trinidad and Tobago.

**Beverages**
Like many places throughout the Caribbean, rum is the most popular choice of alcoholic beverage. For something less strong, fruit juices make a pleasant choice, because they are often freshly squeezed from local produce.

Some visitors consider culinary exploration and indulgence a main attraction of a vacation, while others think eating is what you do if there's enough time between surfing and fishing. No matter how you view food, dining on Trinidad and Tobago is a treat for your palate. With a wide range of restaurants that are affordable, as well as an abundant amount of fine dining locales, both active and relaxed travelers alike should be able to enjoy the fruits of this twin-island paradise without problem.

## Trinidadian Culinary Styles

Trinidad and Tobago have been influenced by cultures from around the world, which lends local cuisine a flavorful blend of international style.

"Locals" come from all over, including India, China, Europe, and other parts of the Caribbean. Vacationers will find food on Trinidad and Tobago to be as multi-cultural and diverse as the ethnicity of the people who live here.

When dining on the islands, you will taste that the versatile culinary background is highly influenced by Indian cuisine. Trinidad and Tobago have been influenced by Indian culture more than any other islands in the Caribbean, especially when it comes to food. Spicy curry dishes can be tasted on both islands. *Rotis*, a fiery Indian dish of breads stuffed with chickpea curry and ground meat, is a favorite lunch meal among locals and tourists. You can cool the fire with ice-cold rum punch. Trini's have taken it upon themselves to adapt the *rotis*, creating a variety of similar dishes, such as paratha, dosti, and dhalpourie, which are made with yellow lentils; and aloopourie, made with sweet potatoes.

Spanish culture also has influenced Trinidad and Tobago's cuisine and is seen in tasty Creole dishes such as Pelau, the islands' national dish, a meal of rice, peas, and meat, bear a Spanish stamp. When African slaves were brought to the islands, their food and cuisine also blended with other styles, bringing root vegetables such as yams and dasheen to the table. You'll also find Chinese food almost everywhere on the islands. Local seafood specials like chip chip, a clam-like shellfish, and stuffed crabs are popular among visitors to the islands. More adventurous eaters try the armadillo and possum stew.

However, travelers should not assume that the only foods will be Spanish or Indian. The African slaves brought their own cuisines to the island. Caribbean style fare (which is usually quite heavily influenced by African foods) is also widely available. No matter what flavors you're looking for, Trinbagonians can offer you incredible flavors.

Food is a major part of the people of Trinidad and Tobago's culture, and Trinbagonians enjoy eating good foods while socializing with friendly people. Visitors can learn a lot about the islands through the cuisine alone, and many are in awe of the smörgåsbord of **restaurants** that are available. Trinidad and Tobago has some of the widest varieties of dining establishments in the Caribbean, which ranges from upscale restaurants to small family eateries and roadside vendors. Deciding where to dine may be one of the most difficult choices you will make on your island getaway.

Vegetarians may enjoy offerings of roadside vendors. Doubles are a yummy vegetarian sandwich popular among vegetarians and meat-eaters alike. The sandwich is made up of curried chickpeas surrounded by two rounds of fried dough, which can be enjoyed any time of day.

Below is a sampling of some of Trinidad and Tobago's stand out dishes:

## Trinidad

- Bake and shark - shark meat topped with various relishes and sandwiched between two slices of fried bread;
- Buljol - shredded saltfish mixed with onions, tomatoes and olive oil;
- Callaloo - soup consisting of dasheen leaves, coconut milk, ochroes, and pumpkin, sometimes salted meat or crab is added;
- Chip chip - tiny curried shell fish;
- Chokas - roasted and pounded vegetables;
- Coconut jelly - meat scooped directly from the coconut;
- Creole corn soup - thick and creamy soup loaded up with corn and other vegetables;
- Fruit chow - chopped fruit (half ripe to ripe), and mixed with lime juice, pepper, salt, oil, cilantro, and garlic;
- Pastel - meat, lentils or soya with olives, raisins, and capers encased in cornmeal and steamed in banana leaves;
- Pelau - meat, rice, and pigeon peas;
- Pholourie - fritters made of flour and split peas, topped with chutney;
- Sanoche - split pea, dumpling, carrots, meat, and ground provisions soup;

➢ Souse - boiled pig trotters or chicken feet, chilled and served in a brine of pepper, onions, cucumbers, and lime;

Now that you know all about Trinidad and Tobago's delectable offerings, you're probably chomping at the bit, ready to begin your vacation and sample as much as you can. By visiting our Restaurant Directory, you may search restaurants by name, or if you are interested in a particular cuisine, See Food page.

Reading descriptions of the island's restaurants will give you a better idea of where you want to eat when you arrive. If you are still undecided where to stay, you can learn about restaurants at specific hotels in several ways. First, consider visiting our article listing the Best Hotels for Dining Options. Or, select hotels that interest you from our extensive list (A to Z: Hotels in Detail), and read about their restaurants, as well as other nearby dining options within our detailed discussion of each property.

Travelers will be able to choose from Chinese, Lebanese, French, Italian, Indian, and Thai foods along with many other diverse dishes while on the island, so no matter what kind of food you're craving, Trinidad and Tobago can cater to the most discerning of tastes.

## Restaurants on Trinidad

## Restaurants on Trinidad represent a variety of cultures

While restaurants may not be easy to come by in undeveloped and less traveled parts of the islands, Trinidad's restaurants showcases international and local cuisine.

Many cultures have effected island cuisine. Large populations of residents who come from other parts of the world have settled on Trinidad and brought with them many different kinds of foods. Chinese food, for example, is widely available and popular, as is Indian food. The Spanish controlled Trinidad until the end of the 18th century, and Spanish influences can still be tasted in local cuisine. When you throw in African and indigenous Caribbean culinary influences, you wind up with a very flavorful way of cooking. To learn about all of Trinidad and culinary treats, visit our guide to Culinary Styles on the islands. Fast food establishments and street and beach vendors remain one of the most popular ways to get a meal on the island. Vendors should have food badges declaring that they comply with health regulations.

Restaurants on Trinidad are largely unpretentious and located in old houses and buildings along the ocean or in tourist areas. Beachwear is never considered appropriate in most restaurants in the Caribbean. Dinner dress generally consists of trousers and a collared or button-down shirt for men, and informal dresses for women. Travelers should be comfortable and casual but neat while enjoying the delicious food of the islands. Travelers who have business in restaurants meetings may want to call ahead to check on dress codes.

Reservations in upscale restaurants, tourist areas, and in Port of Spain are always recommended during high season, and in the busy time around Carnival. Although reservations are needed at some restaurants, street vendors and bake stands allow hungry travelers to eat on a whim. Check out our Restaurant Directory to search restaurants by name, or if you are interested in a particular cuisine, click here to find contact information.

If you are still undecided where to stay, you can learn about restaurants at specific hotels in several ways. First, consider visiting our article listing the Best Hotels for Dining Options. Or, select hotels that interest you from our extensive list (A to Z: Hotels in Detail), and read about their restaurants, as well as other nearby dining options within our detailed discussion of each property.

On top of taxes, restaurants generally add a 10 to 15 percent service charge to your check. If this service charge is not included, a tip equal to this amount is considered appropriate. For travelers who feel they have received exceptional service, an extra percentage is recommended and appreciated.

Dining can be an important and memorable part of any trip to the Caribbean. The flavors and restaurants on Trinidad represent a number of cultures throughout the world and give vacationers an opportunity to relax in peaceful and quiet environments while enjoying the cuisine.

RESTAURANTS BY CUISINE

| Cuisine | Restaurants | Locations |
| --- | --- | --- |
| American | 36 Restaurants | Chaguanas, Woodbrook, St. James, Montrose, Sangre Grande, Arima, Chaguaramas, San Juan, San Fernando, Port of Spain, downtown Port of Spain, Trinidad, Siparia, the vicinity of Port of Spain, Valsayn |
| Asian | 3 Restaurants | downtown Port of Spain, the vicinity of Port of Spain |
| Asian Fusion | 1 Restaurant | downtown Port of Spain |
| Brazilian | 1 Restaurant | Port of Spain |
| Caribbean | 21 Restaurants | St. Ann's, Woodbrook, Cascade, Claxton Bay, Chaguaramas, Blanchisseuse, Maracas Bay, Port of Spain, downtown Port of Spain, Trinidad, the vicinity of Port of Spain, San Fernando, Valsayn |
| Chinese | 48 Restaurants | Chaguanas, San Fernando, Mac Bean, Green Turtle Cay, Princes Town, St. Clair, Arima, Woodbrook, Port of Spain, Debe, Trinidad, |

|  |  | Valsayn, Siparia, the vicinity of Port of Spain, Maraval |
| --- | --- | --- |
| Creole | 3 Restaurants | Woodbrook, downtown Port of Spain, Trinidad |
| French | 3 Restaurants | St. James, Port of Spain, Trinidad |
| Fusion | 3 Restaurants | Woodbrook, Maracas Bay, Port of Spain |
| Indian | 5 Restaurants | Chaguanas, Woodbrook, San Fernando, downtown Port of Spain, Maraval |
| International | 28 Restaurants | Chaguanas, Claxton Bay, Maracas Bay, Cascade, Trinidad, Chaguaramas, Woodbrook, Port of Spain, D'abadie, the vicinity of Port of Spain, San Fernando, Maraval |
| Italian | 32 Restaurants | Montrose, Woodbrook, St. Augustine, Sangre Grande, Gasparillo, San Juan, St. Ann's, Port of Spain, Trinidad, Valsayn, San Fernando, the vicinity of Port of Spain |
| Jamaican | 1 Restaurant | San Fernando |
| Japanese | 3 Restaurants | Woodbrook, the vicinity of Port of Spain |
| Mediterranean | 1 Restaurant | St. Ann's |
| Middle Eastern | 2 Restaurants | Woodbrook, Maraval |
| Polynesian | 1 Restaurant | downtown Port of Spain |
| Tex-Mex | 3 Restaurants | Woodbrook, Port of Spain, the vicinity of Port of Spain |

| | | |
|---|---|---|
| Thai | 2 Restaurants | Chaguanas, Belmont |
| Trinidadian | 2 Restaurants | Woodbrook, Trinidad |
| Contemporary | 1 Restaurant | downtown Port of Spain |
| Eclectic | 5 Restaurants | Chaguanas, Woodbrook, the vicinity of Port of Spain, downtown Port of Spain, Maraval |

# Maps Description of Trinidad

## Trinidad and Tobago Maps

Trinidad and Tobago are located in the southern portion of the Caribbean Sea, just off the northeast coast of Venezuela. The archipelago is comprised of the two main islands and 21 small satellite islands that are covered in dense vegetation.

Both of the major islands are covered in rivers, streams and luscious tropical forests. Trinidad has a mountaineous area along the northern coast, with a landscape that is more reminiscent of some South American destinations than the typical Caribbean island. Both Trinidad and Tobago offer ideal vacation spots for those who love to explore the outdoors. If necessary, just widen your browser to view the entire map.

## Attractions

Trinidad is home to a number of attractions that will dazzle tourists. At the Botanic Gardens near Port of Spain toward the center of the map, guests can spend their afternoon exploring the sprawling grounds of this natural haven. If you're interested in scoping out the history of Trinidad, head over to the Queen's Park Savannah and the Magnificent Seven. Also located in the Port of Spain, this area showcases a collection of Victorian architecture, including a museum and the prime minister's office.

Just south of Port of Spain, the Caroni Bird Sanctuary boasts magnificent views and bird watching for creatures like the country's national bird, the Scarlet Ibis. For another encounter with nature, check out the Asa Wright Nature Centre in northern Trinidad, near Arima.

If you decide to visit Tobago, you'll find a wide range of things to do and see. At the Tobago Forest Reserve, tourists can adventure through the oldest rain forest reserve in the entire western hemisphere. The park offers guided tours and plentiful hiking trails through the jungle terrain. The Fort King George in Scarborough provides guests with a breathtaking attraction that combines architecture and nature with a fort that is delicately perched on a towering cliff-side. The Tobago Museum is located nearby, and is home to many artifacts like ancient weapons and maps. Just off the northeast coast of Tobago, the island of Little Tobago makes for a great day trip for anyone keen on admiring the outdoor beauty in its unspoiled state.

The beaches of Trinidad and Tobago are probably the nation's most popular attractions. On the island of Trinidad, the most frequented beaches are found along the northern coast, including the popular Blanchisseuse beach and secluded Macqueripe Bay. Farther south, some of the best beaches include the family-friendly shores of Quinam Beach and the sunbather's paradise at Manzanilla Beach.

The island of Tobago boasts equally enticing beaches in a much more compact area, including its most famous location at Pigeon Point, where vacationers can enjoy water sports, swimming and a glass bottom boat tour. The best snorkeling on Tobago can be found at Mt. Irvine beach on the Leeward Coast, where beach-goers can also rent canoes and other water sport equipment.

## Places to Stay

### Trinidad
The larger of the two islands, Trinidad offers multiple places to stay. In the general vicinity of Port of Spain on the map, you'll find a good variety of accommodation options. This area appeals to guests

wanting to stay close to the action -- it features a good variety of dining options, as well as shopping opportunities and attractions like the Magnificent Seven. If you're most interested in spending time soaking up the sun, and prefer a less populated area, consider staying near Blanchisseuse. This area is also home to a good selection of accommodations, one of the nation's top beaches, and turtle nesting grounds. Additional lodging facilities can be found in several other locations on Trinidad -- for instance, near Chaguaramas and in the area east of Matelot.

## Tobago

The largest concentration of accommodations on Tobago are centered around the city of Scarborough. The area is home to a large number of restaurants and shopping, as well as dozens of lodging facilities. But, as you venture farther out along both coasts, you will encounter additional accommodations, ranging from resorts and hotels to rental villas and condos. The southernmost tip of the island, near Canaan on the map, also features lodging facilities, restaurants, sight-seeing opportunities and more. Those interested in staying on the northern end of Tobago will find another concentration of lodging in the area near Charlotteville.

## Transportation

Each of the twin islands features its own airport. In Trinidad, the Piarco International Airport (POS) is located on the northern end of Trinidad, a bit southeast of the c ity of Port of Spain. This facility serves flights arriving from the United States, Canada, Venezuela and other parts of the Caribbean. Tobago's airport, the Crown Point Airport (TAB), is situated near the town of Canaan. It serves flights from Trinidad and several other Caribbean islands, as well as mainland destinations as far away as London and New York.

Both Trinidad and Tobago are equipped with their own cruise ports. Vacationers visiting Trinidad on a cruise ship will generally dock at the Cruise Ship Complex in the Port of Spain. This dock features duty-free shopping, clothing boutiques and a Tourism Information Office for travelers. In Tobago, most ships arrive at the cruise terminal in the city of Scarborough. This dock houses an ice cream shop, market vendors, a Tourism Information Office and more.

Travel by ferry is a popular option for vacationers wanting to see both islands. The Trinidad-Tobago Ferry transports passengers on large catamarans between locations in Port of Spain and Scarborough. Another alternative is the Trinidad & Tobago Inter-Island Transportation Company, which provides similar services between these same two cities.

# Planning Your Vacation on Trinidad

## Research will help you plan the trip of a lifetime

From a festive Carnival to unspoiled natural preserves, Trinidad and Tobago have much to offer vacationers. The beauty of the islands' beaches and forests is a main attraction for visitors. Research all your possibilities to be sure you make the most of your experience on the islands.

Vacationers who are traveling to Trinidad and Tobago have the added challenge of choosing between two islands. With so many options available on either island, travelers should be sure to consider the type of vacation they wish to take, who they will travel with, how they will budget the trip, and when they will go. All this should be firmly decided before making final arrangements for their trip.

**Getting Info**

Travelers have many different resources to consult while conductingresearch, from friends and coworkers, to books and Internet sites. Business directories may give you a list of local recreational vendors from which to rent scuba and snorkeling equipment or . Start here with our comprehensive guides on everything from culture to food, and allow your research to progress from there.

**Making Decisions**

With such a large variety of settings and accommodations, Trinidad and Tobago can provide a number of different experiences. The islands can be romantic, relaxing, and exciting all at once. Choose your hotel accommodations and activities based on the type of trip you want. For romance, consider an isolated beach villa or inn on Tobago. Families looking for relaxation may prefer an , while eco-adventurers have great options for staying on either island.

**Booking Your Trip**

Booking your travel can now be done easily through the Internet, and many Internet sites offer significantly reduced rates on airfare and accommodations. Travel agents and phone representatives are other options. Vacationers should always make sure to consider climate and seasonal events before embarking upon the final booking process.

Proper planning and research can help you build a vacation that fulfills all your expectations and ensures you will find the right accommodations and activities when you visit Trinidad and Tobago.

# Booking your Trip to Trinidad

Choose a method of booking your travel that you are comfortable with

Many methods of travel booking are available, but most travelers find the Internet an easy and convenient way to search deals and make their final reservations. But travel agents or telephone reservations are also effective ways to make your arrangements. Use whichever method that inspires the most confidence for you.

For those interested in visiting Trinidad and Tobago, several options are available. The Internet allows you to search and review, without deadlines or pressure, deals and special offers on airfare, accommodations, car rentals, and activities. You can easily compare sites against each other, then book your final arrangements on sites that guarantee security.

Phone contact provides human interaction, and working directly with a company usually means you can be clear about your preferences, and you can understand companies' policies and fees by asking direct questions about them. Travel agents and Internet travel vendors, meanwhile, can be useful in holding companies accountable for bad service. It is in the best interest of travel vendors and travel agents to use only the services that consistently satisfy their customers. Travel vendors and travel agents can drop services and companies that can lower their reputation by providing bad services to customers.

Internet travel vendors are one of the most popular means of booking travel. These sites offer databases of large amounts of collected information concerning services and amenities in air travel, hotels, transportation, cruises, and other services. Travelers can review a long list of options of varying prices and types of services, along with a list of benefits for booking with each. Some sites also sell packages that can include airfare, hotels, rental cars, and activities all in one price.

Those looking through travel vendor sites should be able to find both travel vendors that focus on general travel throughout the globe, as well as travel within the Caribbean region itself. Travelers may wish to consult both types of sites in their research in order to search out the best deals. Many of these sites will have prices that are very similar to one another, as the deals that are offered to the various sites directly from vendors will not vary greatly. Always be sure, however, to be sure of what is included in the price you are being quoted, as taxes, service charges, and convenience fees may drive up your price at a later step. Some airlines may also include island departure or arrival taxes in their airfare, and this is also a factor to consider when looking at their prices.

For travelers who prefer to go directly through a vendor, many hotels and airlines and even rental car agencies allow you to book online directly through their Web sites. Companies will often offer special electronic booking deals to customers who secure their reservations through the Internet.

Although the secure websites used by travel vendors and companies online generally make it very safe to book your travel over the Internet, there are many travelers who still feel uncomfortable with using the Internet. Some find the idea of electronically transmitting data such as personal information and credit card numbers over the Internet to be discomforting. Travel agents and phone contact are two other ways of securing travel for those who feel this insecure about electronic booking.

Some people prefer to be able to have personal contact with representatives from a company in order to be able to ask questions. Contacting travel and accommodation companies directly over the phone can allow travelers to speak to a representative who can answer such questions about policies and fees as the booking process takes place. Phone representatives may be able to offer travelers reduced rates on services, but these are generally not as significant as the discounts offered through Internet specials. When making such a significant purchase such as travel arrangements, however, it never hurts to explore all of the options that are available to you.

Travel agents are a final way of booking your travel and can offer packaged deals to destinations throughout the world and Caribbean. People who are familiar with a particular travel agent may find a sense of trust in working with another person who is knowledgeable about a destination such as Trinidad and Tobago. Many people may continually go back to the same travel agent, and establish a friendly relationship in which the travel agent understands your wants and wishes for the types of vacations that you take. Travel agents who do not specialize in the Caribbean, however, may not be able to offer you extensive information without conducting additional research.

Researching and booking your travel is very important for travelers to find the types of services that will help them enjoy their vacation. Consider your options for booking a vacation to Trinidad and Tobago, and choose a good deal from a reputable and knowledgeable source.

# Budgeting

How Much Will it Cost to Vacation on Trinidad?
**When planning a vacation, travelers should keep their finances in mind**
Before you get swept away in the sea of possibilities that await you on Trinidad and Tobago, it's a good idea to plan your budget. If you have at least a general idea of what you are spending, you will reduce the

number of surprise expenses and will be able to relax more completely once you arrive on these lovely sister islands.

Having an educated estimate of your expenses is an important part of getting the most from your vacation. The majority of your budget will be the costs of accommodations and transportation, but remember to budget for smaller expenses, such as meals, sightseeing tours, souvenirs, and taxes, which can add up and become significant in the end.

**Accommodations**

The cost of your accommodations will depend on the time of year you visit the islands, the type of lodging you choose, and the location of your accommodations. Vacationers have several options when choosing a hotel, from small guesthouses, eco-lodges and inns to luxurious all-inclusive megaresorts. When deciding on accommodations, you should choose a place that best reflects your budget and your vacation style.

Trinidad and Tobago's beautiful rainforests and natural sites make the islands great places for campers and nature lovers. Travelers wanting to spend time enjoying the natural beauty of the island will find that camping grounds and eco-lodgings are highly affordable, starting as low as $25(USD). Vacationers who want to spend the least amount on accommodations but don't necessarily want to spend time in the great outdoors can also find inexpensive rooms starting at approximately $20(USD) per night. For more exquisite lodgings that offer lavish amenities, tourists can pay more for luxury rooms, which can cost approximately $300(USD) or more per night. Many hotels and resorts provide all-inclusive packages that allow vacationers to pay for many aspects of their stay with one bill, which can be convenient and cost-effective for many travelers. A stay in an all-inclusive hotel or resort starts at about $250(USD). Keep in mind that these prices don't include government taxes and any services charges.

The time of year you travel will also influence vacation costs, particularly what you pay for accommodations. During the high tourist season, which is from December to April, prices are considerably higher in the Caribbean. If you want to save significant amounts of money, consider traveling during the off season, when fewer tourists visit the islands and hotel and resort prices drop.

**Daily Spending**

Worldwide culinary influences have produced a dynamic local cuisine, making dining a top priority for most visitors. Meals are a basic necessity, so be sure to budget generously for dining during your vacation. Restaurants, however, are ample, which means you can dine on a flexible budget on Trinidad and Tobago. In fact, dining on the islands is very affordable compared to some vacation destinations in the Caribbean.

The most inexpensive meals come from street vendors, which sell local delicacies like tasty Doubles, a fried, curried chickpea sandwich that is a popular choice among vegetarians. Most of the restaurants on the island are very casual, and their prices are very affordable. Travelers can pay as little as $1(USD) for a tasty meal. Dishes at more upscale restaurants cost a little bit more, and travelers can expect to pay around $40(USD) per meal.

Gratuity should be a part of your budget. Tipping is not required on Trinidad and Tobago, but generally vacationers tip 10 to 15 percent for good service. Many people in the service industry rely heavily on tips and gratuities as a majority of their income. Tipping is a good way to reward a service well done.

How you get around once you arrive on Trinidad or Tobago is also going to have to be part of your budget. Some methods of transportation are more costly than others. There are many ways to see the islands, from public transportation to ferries. Choose whichever method fits your lifestyle.

At $2(TT), or approximately $0.32(USD), per ticket, minibuses are one of the cheapest ways to tour both Trinidad and Tobago. Taxis are another popular form of inexpensive transportation around the islands. They may cost a little more than riding the bus, but taxis allow you to see Trinidad and Tobago on your own terms. Cab fare varies depending on your destination, but generally starts at approximately $5(USD).

Rental cars are the most expensive way to get around the islands, but many vacationers feel the independence of driving themselves is well worth the cost. The cost of renting a car depends on the vehicle and the rental company you choose, but rates usually start at approximately $70(USD).

Travelers may want to travel between Trinidad and Tobago, and inter-island ferry service is available during the week and on Sundays. Ferries generally take approximately five hours one way, and costs start at $50(TT) or about $8.04(USD) per ticket. Children under 12 ride for half price.

There may be other incidental costs for daily spending such as museum admissions or night club covers and drinks that vacationers may want to consider when budgeting. Although you may not be able to budget every cost of your daily spending, estimating will allow you to approximate how much you will need.

## Shopping

Vacationers will find some of the largest bazaars in the Caribbean located on the two islands, which sell international items from Ireland, Scandinavia, and Japan, to name a few. Handmade crafts are also popular, and many people enjoy exploring the fun shops for souvenirs.

While you may find good deals on merchandise while on Trinidad and Tobago, vacationers should keep in mind that their purchases may incur taxes when returning through customs. Travelers should check with their home country's customs office to find out which items are duty-free and which are taxed.

## Taxes

All travelers visiting Trinidad and Tobago under the age of 60 are subject to a departure tax of $100(TT), which is about $16(USD), when leaving the country. This tax goes to the country's government and is used to meet the development costs of the country. Often this cost is included with the cost of your plane ticket, but check with your airline to be sure.

Hotels apply a 15 percent value added tax to all final hotel bills, and most implement a 10 percent service charge as well. Vacationers should check ahead of time to see whether these fees are included with the costs of their room. Planning a budget for your vacation is a helpful way to get the most out of your trip to Trinidad and Tobago and to avoid many unexpected surprises.

## Getting Info

### Getting More Info Concerning Trinidad
**Let research get you excited about your vacation**
Whether you are traveling to buzzing Trinidad or staying amid the natural beauty of Tobago, there are many ways to collect information about the two islands. Use careful research and planning to craft a vacation that meets all your expectations.

Many people often first hear about an island from friends or co-workers, and these primary firsthand contacts make excellent resources as you begin to plan your trip. Knowing someone familiar with your own tastes can go a long way in discovering must-see sites, off-tourist-path secrets, and restaurants that serve the freshest local dishes.

More and more travelers are turning to the Internet to conduct their research and book travel. Consult the Internet at any time during your planning, and you will discover the online community is an irreplaceable tool for information about Trinidad and Tobago. Use this site as an extensive and easy-to-navigate resource for learning about Trinidad and Tobago. Travelers can learn about everything from driving conditions and rental properties to health and safety tips to yachting information. The Official Tourism Website of Trinidad and Tobago (http://www.visittnt.com/) can also be a good resource for learning general and travel information concerning the island. Travelers can also access brochures and request feedback while navigating the site. The Caribbean Tourism Organization (http://www.onecaribbean.org/) can also provide additional information to travelers.

Once these resources have been exhausted, consider other online options for accessing and reviewing information about Trinidad and Tobago. A search engine such as Google will yield a long list of sites of varying reliability and information. Use caution when consulting personal sites because information may not always be accurate. If you have questions regarding information found on a site that does not seem official, the tourism board could be a good contact for verifying whatever you find.

You are sure to come across Internet vendor travel sites that can research and book hotels, flights, and transportation online. Sites such as these allow travelers to see a long list of available amenities and benefits that come with each service. Travelers can access these sites early in their research to learn what options will be suitable for the type of vacation they wish to plan. Travelers looking for all-inclusive resorts can discover the offerings of various locations and companies, while eco-tourists can learn which regions and accommodations cater to an adventurous vacation and lifestyle. Once you have conducted additional research, you can always return to these sites to book your final travel arrangements.

Travelers can also access Web sites of various travel magazines, which often maintain a searchable electronic database of past articles and features on the Caribbean and specific islands. Internet researchers can also procure phone and business directories, which help locate companies that offer jet ski rentals, dentists, or any imagineable type of service. Phone numbers, addresses, and even Web sites of both large and small and locally owned businesses should be available through these sites.

Internet message and bulletin boards are a final option for researchers on the Internet and are another way of learning other traveler's opinions and reflections on Trinidad and Tobago. If you are interested in a particular hotel or resort, tourist site, or restaurant, look for reviews and posts by other travelers who have been to the island. See what others are saying about taking the ferry from Trinidad to Tobago. These boards are a popular way for researchers to post questions and receive responses from people who have been to the islands. Whether you read through past Q and A's or post a new question yourself, be aware that the people posting information on these boards are not official sources, and information might be misleading or inaccurate. Always attempt to verify information you receive with official sources, and never disclose personal information over the Internet.

If your Internet search has not exhausted you, visit a bookstore or library to consult travel guides for the Caribbean and Trinidad and Tobago. General Caribbean guides can help familiarize you with the region while guides written specifically about Trinidad and Tobago will supply detailed information and essential facts and tips. Many different Caribbean and Trinidad and Tobago guidebooks are available. Take time to browse through a number of them. Some guides may feature extensive listings for all-inclusive resorts and fine dining, while others may be good sources for eco-adventure. Travelers might also consider purchasing a book to have a handy, physical resource during the vacation.

Several magazines found in your local bookstore can be a good source for feature articles about Trinidad and Tobago. Magazines may also have advertising and contact information for local businesses on your island of choice.

Travelers who take time to research and plan their trip usually reap the relaxing benefits of being knowledgeable about their destination. Take some time to learn more about Trinidad and Tobago by consulting any of the various sources of information that are available.

# Making Decisions

## How to Decide What You Want for your Vacation on Trinidad

**Make decisions based on your own vacation ideals**

In order to get the most out of a trip to Trinidad and Tobago, make travel decisions based on the type of vacation you want to have. People visit this region for different reasons, so choosing appropriate itineraries and accommodations means your vacation will be an enjoyable one.

**Narrow Your Search (Which place is best for me?)**

Once you have decided to plan a trip to Trinidad and Tobago, you should begin to think about where you want to stay. Trinidad and Tobago have a rich Caribbean culture, great shopping, beautiful beaches, and eco-adventures. For a vacation defined by city life and shopping, you may wish to stay near Port of Spain on Trinidad. Those interested in the flora and fauna of the islands may want to look into staying in the northeast area of Trinidad where the Asa Wright Nature Centre allows visitors to get close to up to 400 species of birds. Although the island is small, deciding where to stay can be important for organizing your activities and day trips.

Travelers who want to stretch out on the beach should consider staying on Tobago. The less developed of the islands offers travelers much in the form of eco-adventure, from snorkeling and scuba diving to hiking. Although an increase in development has brought more tourists, the beauty of the island continues to attract those looking for retreat in natural settings.

Although natural beauty is found on both islands, the type of activities you wish to pursue can help you decide where to stay. Different areas cater to different travelers. Yachting enthusiasts may wish to stay around Chaguaramas on Trinidad, while those who are interested in snorkeling and scuba diving may choose Tobago's southwest coast, among other places.

**Arrivals (How will I get there?)**
Travelers to Trinidad and Tobago can choose air or sea travel to get to the islands. Flying is a fast and popular way of traveling to all destinations in the Caribbean, and Trinidad's international airport

handles an impressive flow of visitor traffic, but Tobago also has a smaller airport. If you want to see Trinidad and Tobago, ferry service shuttles passengers between the islands.

Travelers arriving by sea usually enjoy the journey as much as arriving at their destination. Although Trinidad and Tobago are tucked into the Southern rim of the Caribbean, many cruise lines call on the islands.

Travelers to the island should also consider their means of transportation once they arrive. Those looking to tour extensively on either island may find it beneficial to rent a car rather than pay taxi or bus fares.

## On the Island (Where will I go on the island?)

Once you have decided where to stay, start thinking about what you want to do and where you want to go. Consider which activities interest you most, which will require reservations, and which day trips, if any, you want to take.

If you are traveling alone, with a friend, or as a couple, you may be interested in more adventurous, outgoing activities such as eco-adventures, hikes, and mountain-biking tours. Families with younger children may want to consider visiting nature preserves or museums. Some may prefer the quiet of a small seaside villa, while others may prefer an all-inclusive resort experience.

Regardless of where you stay on the island and what activities you plan, it's a good idea to explore the many offerings of Trinidad and Tobago. Quiet beaches, lush flora, exotic fauna, and plenty of culture give travelers many options during their stay. Plan a day trip in your itinerary to do something a little different or be spontaneous during your stay.

No matter what kind of trip you wish to have and where you end up staying on the island, Trinidad and Tobago offer travelers beauty and culture. Proper planning and decision-making will help ensure you make the most out of your vacation to the islands

# Packing

## What Should You Pack for a Trip to Trinidad?
**Planning what to pack for your vacation on Trinidad and Tobago requires a little forethought**
The thing about packing for a vacation on Trinidad and Tobago is that many people make it out to be harder than it actually is.

By taking the time to learn about the weather and determine what clothing would be most appropriate for the activities you will participate in, you'll have a good idea of everything that will need to be put in your luggage.

**First and Foremost**

Entering Trinidad and Tobago is pretty simple if you plan to stay less than three months; all that is required of you is a passport and a return or ongoing ticket to show customs officials that you plan to exit the islands by a certain date. A smart plan of action would be to make copies of both of these items, as well as your government issued identification card and pack them away in your checked luggage. This way, if the originals are lost or stolen you have a backup.

Keeping cash on hand as you travel from your hometown to Trinidad and Tobago is a good idea. Even though you may prefer to use credit cards when you travel overseas, there is always a chance that the credit card machines will be down, or the place you are at only accepts cash. The official currency on Trinidad and Tobago is the Trinidad and Tobago Dollar.

A few other important things to keep on your person as you travel include prescription slips for any medications that you are bringing with you to the islands, a list of emergency contacts, and paperwork documenting your hotel, rental car, and pre-planned activities reservations.

**Clothing**
The islands in the Caribbean are hot, and Trinidad and Tobago, with their close proximity to the equator, are some of the hottest. This is

why it is imperative that you pack clothes that will keep you cool and comfortable. These items come in the form of natural fabrics, such as cotton, and should be light-weight, and light in color. Linen or khaki shorts are preferable for your bottom half, and t-shirts or tank tops will keep you cool up top. Protect your feet by surrounding them in comfortable athletic shoes or hiking boots.

**Formal Wear**
It is unlikely that you will be required to wear formal clothing at any time during your vacation, unless you have a business meeting, event, or special dinner planned. If you do need something more formal than your day wear, men should pack the following items: collared shirts, slacks, closed toed shoes, and perhaps a sports jacket. For women, a nice pants suit, sun dress, or a cocktail dress with the appropriate jewelry and shoes.

**Swim Wear**
The beaches of Trinidad and Tobago are hard to resist, and even if you don't care to splash around in the surf, you can hang out at your hotel's pool. For these activities, of course, you will need at least one swimsuit. You may even want to consider bringing more than one. This way you can leave one in your hotel room to dry while you wear the other out for the day.

Your revealing swim wear should not come away from the beach or pool, however. Bring along a cover-up, such as a sarong or cover-up for the times when you need to run into a gift shop or want to grab a bite to eat.

Sun hats, sun glasses, and flip flops or sandals are essential pieces to bring along as well. Don't forget sunscreen!

**Toiletries and Health Care**
Any item that you consider to be an important part of your daily routine can come with you on your trip. Dental hygiene, hair care products, and other body care items all fall into this category. To save space, pick up travel sized versions of these products, and pack them in a bag specifically for your toiletries so there is no chance they will leak onto your other belongings..

Take precaution when it comes to bugs. Mosquitoes can be a problem, so pack bug repellent, as well as hydrocortisone cream or Benadryl to offer relief if you are in fact bit..

**What Else to Pack**
Nights can become chilly on Trinidad and Tobago. A sweater or a wrap are great to have on hand after the sun sets, so be sure to pack something a little warmer than your day clothes. Rain is another issue to be concerned with. A rain jacket, poncho, or umbrella will provide

you with the protection you need to enable you to forge ahead with your outdoor exploration efforts.

For your down time, you'll want to bring along something to entertain yourself. Now-a-days electronics are popular choices: e-readers, mp3 players, portable DVD players, laptops, and hand held video game systems are often brought along on vacation. You can also bring a book, journal, deck of cards, or other travel game.

When you bring electronics, remember to pack enough batteries, or the power supply cord with you. Some hotels on Trinidad and Tobago have the same outlets as are common in the United States, while others offer adapters free-of-charge to guests. Call your hotel to find out if you will need to bring your own adapters.

Also, remember to pack your camera, as well as the equipment you need to keep it running and an extra memory card.
One thing you definitely won't want to forget is your camera, and everything you need to keep your camera up and running. An extra memory card is desirable as well..

**Packing Concerns**
If you are visiting Trinidad and Tobago for an extended period of time, or simply worried about packing too much, consider this trip from travel experts: pack items that are interchangeable, and can be worn a

number of ways while still looking fresh. A pair of cloth shorts, for example, will go nicely with a variety of shirts, and a selection of colored shirts can be layered differently each day for a new look.

Some vacationers worry that their luggage will get lost or delayed by the airline when they fly to the island. Although this occurrence is rare, you can arrive prepared for this possibility. Include in your carry on bag one outfit and a swim suit, along with any small, but valuable items, and medications that are necessary for you to take. This way, you will have a few essential items available to you immediately, and you can shop for the rest when you arrive on Trinidad and Tobago.

Attack your suitcase with a plan of action. By determining what activities you'll be participating in, taking the weather into account, and writing out a list of everything you want to have with you, packing for Trinidad and Tobago will be a breeze.

## Best Time to Visit

When is the Best Time to Visit Trinidad?
**Both the low and high Caribbean seasons offer advantages to travelers**
Whether you go to enjoy Port of Spain, bird watching, or eco-adventures, Trinidad and Tobago offer its friendly culture and natural

beauty throughout the year. However, different seasons do affect the kind of vacation you'll have as well as how much it will cost.

Travel to the Caribbean is broken into two seasons, high and low. Although travel to the region is popular throughout the year, each season holds advantages and disadvantages for travelers. The high travel season in the Caribbean is mid-December to mid-April, while the low travel season spans the remainder of the year.

**Weather**

Trinidad and Tobago have two seasons that coincide largely with the high and low travel season. From January to May the islands experiences a dry season with mild temperatures without added precipitation and humidity. From May to December, the island experiences its wet season, with considerably more rainfall and cooler temperatures. Petit Carême occurs between mid-September to mid-October and is a brief cessation of regular rainfall.

The island's average yearly temperature of 82 degrees Fahrenheit coupled with the onset of the dry season gives travelers sufficient reason to vacation on Trinidad and Tobago. When you factor in the frigid weather that destinations in North America and Europe experience in winter, a vacation to the Caribbean and Trinidad and Tobago can be an appealing option for those who want to escape the chill. Although Trinidad and Tobago are typically removed from hurricane paths, the ending of the Atlantic hurricane season at the end of November takes away much of the weather hazard that comes with traveling in the region from June to November.

## High Season on Trinidad and Tobago

Those who choose to travel during the Caribbean high season will certainly have plenty of company. Large numbers of travelers from around the globe will migrate to islands throughout the region. As a result, hotels, restaurants, and businesses will be offering more services and will be running at full capacity. Restaurants may expand their menus and take on extra staff, while and other hotels will generally offer more amenities, such as recreational activities, health and spa services, and classes and instruction for their guests. Bars, clubs, and other social venues will generally be more crowded from the scores of young travelers socializing after a day on the beach. With such large numbers of people traveling to the region during this time, you're wise to secure your flight and hotel reservations at least a few months in advance. Restaurants and other services will also be in high demand, and reservations are recommended.

## Low Season on Trinidad and Tobago

The Caribbean off season still offers much to travelers to Trinidad and Tobago. Although the islands experience a significant increase in rainfall during this time, showers generally occur in the afternoons and may bring with them cooler temperatures. Many hotels, airlines, and other services may reduce their prices during the Caribbean off season up to 50 percent. Travelers should monitor the Atlantic storm and weather systems and also check extended local forecasts for Trinidad and Tobago if they are traveling during this time.

Although many hotels and services might close during the off season, travelers using the ones that remain open should find it considerably easier to make reservations. Some hotels will use the slow season for maintenance and construction on their property, so it pays to ask if any renovations are planned during your visit.

**Festivals and Events**

There are a number of festivals and cultural events that take place on Trinidad and Tobago that can also be appealing for travelers throughout various times of the year. Travelers can always check tourist office calendars for a dates of all festivals and activities.

Carnival, a popular festival throughout the Caribbean, takes place on two consecutive days in February and is full of music, dance, singing, and costumes. Aug. 31 marks the islands' Independence Day, while mid-July to early August marks the Tobago Heritage Festival, celebrating the culture and history of the island.

There are also several important Hindu and Muslim festivals and observances that occur on Trinidad and Tobago, including the Hindu festival of Phagwa, celebrating the harvest; and the Muslim day of Eid-Ul-Fitr, which follows the holy month of Ramadan.

Travelers seeking the pleasures of vacationing on Trinidad and Tobago have options and benefits for traveling during any time of the year.

# Transportation Options for Trinidad

Vacationers can enjoy seeing the island by several means of transportation

Several options for transportation make it easy to get to and around Trinidad. Travelers can choose between cruising, sailing, or flying - and then explore the region by ferry, cab, rental car, or bus.

**Air Travel**

The most popular and convenient way to get to Trinidad is by air. Airports located on the island have scheduled flights to and from most parts of the world. If you are flying into Trinidad, you will arrive at Piarco International Airport near the island's capital, Port of Spain. There are several airlines that have direct flights out of the United

States, Canada, the U.K., and other islands in the Caribbean. To learn some specifics about flying into the island, read on Air Travel page.

**Sailing**

While sailing a private yacht is not the most popular method of transportation, there are a number of things that make sailing to Trinidad preferable. First, it's location below the "hurricane belt" drives insurance costs down, and make yachters feel more comfortable making the trip during hurricane season. Second, the dual island nation has made great strides in improving their docking facilities in recent years, making it one of the best places to dock in the Eastern Caribbean.

Trinidad's main ports are Chaguanas and Port of Spain, both of which are popular tourist destinations and have a lot to offer. At any location, you'll need to be familiar with all of the entry requirements and fees. Read all about them on Sailing & Boating page.

**Cruises**

Vacationers can also sit back and enjoy a luxury cruise en route to Trinidad. Traveling is just as enjoyable as arriving at your destination, and the two islands are increasingly included on cruise routes. There are several ports on both Trinidad where cruise ships may dock though Port of Spain is the most frequently used. This is a great places to dock because of the ability for cruisers to participate in duty free shopping, eat in local restaurants, and find important landmarks is increased due to the high tourism these city's typically see even without cruise ship passengers. See Cruises to find out more about cruising to Trinidad.

**Rental Cars**

For travelers who appreciate their independence and who like to be mobile on a moment's notice, several rental car companies located on the islands can supply you with your own wheels. This option is a little more expensive than some of the other methods of transportation, but renting a car can allow you to create your own vacation on your own schedule and at your own speed.

**Bikes and Mopeds**

A less expensive way to get around independently is to rent a bike or moped. Travelers can experience all the natural beauty of Trinidad's great outdoors while enjoying the mobility and self-sufficiency that bikes and mopeds have to offer. Bike-centric tours of the islands are available regularly, and for those who like to go it alone, there are numerous bike trails of different skill levels known for their whimsical names.

**Taxis**

Taxis are also relatively simple to find and are a good way to leave the driving to someone else. You can find taxi cabs almost anywhere on the island, including airports, cruise ports, and hotels. Taxi cab drivers can also act as tour guides and will happily show you the sites and attractions of Trinidad for an extra cost. More information on taxis can be found on Taxi page in this book.

**Buses**

For traveling long distances on Trinidad, tourists may find that riding the bus is the best way to traverse the island. Buses are generally reliable and easy to use because the color coding of each bus corresponds to its destination. Bus travel is also a great way to experience local **culture**. The wide availability of buses makes them a convenient for vacationers to see and experience the island. Find out more about buses on Buses page.

**Ferries**

Due to the fact that Trinidad and Tobago is a dual island nation, most tourists are relieved to discover that ferry transportion is available between the two islands. This means that guests have the opportunity to explore each island with lowered transportation costs, and have a bit of an adventure along the way. Inter-island ferries are available every day of the week except for Saturday, and even have large enough cargo holds that rental cars can be transported as well.

Traveling around Trinidad should be an enjoyable part of your vacation. Consider your traveling needs to decide which form of transportation is best for you.

## Trinidad Air Travel

### Catching a plane is a fast and convenient way to reach your destination

Trinidad is located at the end of the chain of Caribbean islands. Only a hop from South America, flying is a convenient way to reach this piece of paradise.

Trinidad's Piarco International Airport is located approximately 16 miles from the capital, Port of Spain, and is one of the busiest airports in the Caribbean. This means finding flights will not be that hard.

### Flying to Trinidad from the US

Tourists flying into Trinidad from the United States will have few problems. There are a number of cities that offer direct flights to Trinidad's Piarco International Airport. From the Caribbean Gateway of Miami to as far north as JFK in New York, and as far west as Houston, direct flights are easy to find.

If you're traveling from the states this information may be helpful. Not all of the options you will see listed on some booking engines are good options so it can be helpful to see a summary of which airlines offer direct flights to this location.

| PIARCO INTERNATIONAL AIRPORT U.S. FLIGHTS | | |
|---|---|---|
| To/From | Airport Code | Airlines |
| Fort Lauderdale, FL, USA | FLL | Caribbean Airlines, Jet Blue |
| Miami, FL, USA | MIA | American Airlines, Caribbean Airlines |
| Orlando, FL, USA | MCO | Caribbean Airlines |

## Flying to Trinidad from Canada

Canadian tourists are not as fortunate as their American neighbors. There is currently only one city, Toronto that offers passengers direct flights to Trinidad. Still, since Toronto is not exactly a small town, Canadians should have no problem flying to it from their local airport. Alternatively, you could also fly to one of the American cities above and make a transfer.

## Flying to Trinidad from Europe

Europeans only have one option, London's Gatwick Airport, if they want a direct flight to Trinidad. Not even Frankfurt in Germany offers direct flights. You could also just skip London and take a plane to the United States instead (which is much more common).

If you're flying across the Atlantic the table below is the one you need.

PIARCO INTERNATIONAL AIRPORT EUROPEAN FLIGHTS

| To/From | Airport Code | Airlines |
| --- | --- | --- |
| London, United Kingdom | LGW | Caribbean Airlines |

**Flying to Trinidad from the Caribbean**

The Piarco International Airport serves as a hub of air travel in the Caribbean. There are daily flights to destinations all over the region.

Additionally, and of noticible importance, is the "Sky Bridge" between Trinidad and Tobago. This imaginary bridge symbolizes the air route that connects the two islands that form the nation of Trinidad and Tobago. Flights between the islands occur many times every day via Caribbean Airlines, and only takes 25 minutes.

Check the chart below for a listing of scheduled air service from other Caribbean airports. If you can't take a flight directly from an airport near you, taking a connecting flight from another airport may be a very good solution.

| PIARCO INTERNATIONAL AIRPORT CARIBBEAN FLIGHTS | | |
|---|---|---|
| To/From | Airport Code | Airlines |
| Antigua, Antigua and Barbuda | ANU | LIAT |
| Barbados | BGI | LIAT |
| Calliste, Grenada | GND | Caribbean Airlines, LIAT |
| Castries, Saint Lucia | SLU | Caribbean Airlines, LIAT |
| Kingston, Jamaica | KIN | Caribbean Airlines |
| Simpson Bay, The island of St. Martin and Sint Maarten | SXM | Caribbean Airlines |
| St. Vincent, Saint Vincent and the Grenadines | SVD | LIAT |
| Tobago, Trinidad and Tobago | TAB | Caribbean Airlines |
| Vieux Fort, Saint Lucia | UVF | British Airways |
| Willemstad, Curacao | CUR | LIAT |

## Check out the following table to contact some of the regional air charter companies.

| CHARTER OPERATORS | | | |
|---|---|---|---|
| Name | Phone | Location | Island |

| | | | Trinidad |
|---|---|---|---|
| Abaco Air Charter | (242) 367-2266 | Marsh Harbour | Tobago |
| Aviation Services Of Grenada | (473) 439-0681 | Maurice Bishop Intl Airport - Calliste | Grenada |
| Briko Air Services Ltd | (868) 669-3915 | Piarco - The vicinity of Port of Spain | Trinidad |

## Airport Security

Airlines and airports have increased security measures worldwide, in addition to the standard baggage screening procedures. Be prepared for random security inspections of bags and personal belongings.

Before leaving for the airport, make sure you have your passport and ticket or e-ticket confirmation page readily available. It is a good practice to call the airline in advance to confirm that your flight is scheduled to depart on time.

In order to reduce waiting time and ensure that you reach your gate in a timely manner, consider the following tips to expedite inspection and/or screening:

- ➢ Metal objects will set off detector devices, so passengers should avoid wearing metal items, such as steel-toed boots, heavy jewelry, and large belt buckles.

- ➢ Bring a note from your doctor if you have metal surgical implants to avoid any possible delays.

- ➢ Remember, only ticketed passengers are allowed to pass through security. Check with the airline if you are assisting an elderly person or child for additional regulations.

- ➢ In addition to removing your shoes, jackets and other outerwear, loose change, keys cellular phones and other personal devices will need to be placed in the bin the airport provides for x-ray screening.

The convenience of air travel makes catching a flight to both Trinidad and Tobago a popular way to get to your island vacation.

## Buses on Trinidad

### The color of the bus determines your destination

Regularly scheduled bus services on Trinidad make getting around the islands an easy and affordable way to see as much as you want. Bus routes have many destinations to the majority of the island's cities. Bus stops are usually easy to find, and this method of public transportation is a common way for locals and vacationers to navigate the island.

**Bus Routes**

There are several bus choices available in Port of Spain, the capital city of Trinidad. The minibuses travel from the capital to many of the island's larger towns, and the main departure site is City Gate terminal located on South Quay, where travelers can pick up services to and from Piarco International Airport.

Travelers can find out more information about the buses' running schedules on the west side of the bus platform, where there is an information booth, which is open from 7:00 a.m. to 6:00 p.m. on weekdays and until 12:00 p.m. on Saturdays. Usually this information booth is closed Sundays. Bus passengers can expect to pay about TT$2 to TT$10, depending on the length and destination of the trip.

On Trinidad, buses can be identified by several colors that indicate different destinations. Buses with yellow bands travel around Port of Spain; red-banded buses make stops around eastern Trinidad. Buses with green bands are headed to the southern parts of the island; minibuses featuring black bands are headed for Princes Sound, and buses with brown bands operate between San Fernando and the southwest areas of the island.

Riding the bus on Trinidad is an affordable and reliable way to see the islands and meet locals, while leaving the driving to someone else.

# Trinidad Ferries

## Trinidad is connected to Tobago and other Caribbean islands thanks to ferries

Ferries are not the fastest way to travel to and from Trinidad and Tobago, but it is popular. Many people enjoy taking part in the maritime travel as they chug towards their next destination.

### Riding the Ferries

When it comes to ferries on Trinidad, most people will think only of the connection between Trinidad and Tobago. Luckily, there is hopes that Bedy Oceanliner will add a new service that connects Trinidad to a few other islands. But please note that as of January 2014, the Bedy Oceanliner service has not started. Do not commit to this service before calling and confirming that it is operational.

However, the service to Tobago is full functional and is an iconic feature of the two islands. Many tourist have and will travel between Trinidad and Tobago via the Port Authority ferry. Make no doubts, the ferry is slow, but it serves its purpose.

Port Of Spain Ferry Dock is the only ferry dock in the area. If you want more information, you can call them at (868) 625-4906; you'll find the dock on Wrightson Road just outside the heart of Trinidad.

For those who decide that getting to Tobago is going to be part of their vacation, ferries can be the cheapest option. An adult will have to pay about 37 Trinidad Dollars (about $6 US Dollars) for a one way ticket, while a child will pay half that. See the chart below for more information on rates.

TRINIDAD TO TOBAGO FARES

| Ticket Type | Price on Trinidad Dollars |
|---|---|
| Adult - Cabin | TT $80.00 |
| Adult - Economy | TT $37.50 |
| Child | TT $18.75 |
| Vehicle One Way | TT $150.00 |
| Vehicle Round Trip | TT $250.00 |

FERRY ROUTES, TRINIDAD

| Location Served | Dock A | Dock B | Company | Frequency |
|---|---|---|---|---|
| Port of Spain | Scarborough Ferry Port | Port Of Spain Ferry Dock | Port Authority of Trinidad and Tobago | at least daily |

One other feature to make note of is that the ferry to Tobago also serves as a car barge, so you will be able to bring your car onto the ferry and take it between the islands. However, it is always a good idea to confirm with your rental car agnecy that this is okay with them, as some may have a policy against it.

Regardless, for those who don't mind a slow trek over the water, taking a ferry to Tobago can be a fantastic way to see the islands.

## Trinidad Rental Cars

Travelers looking to tour the islands may wish to rent a car

Although driving in a foreign country can often be an adventurous prospect, cars remain a good option for travelers who will be doing extensive touring of Trinidad.

**Renting a Car**

Rather than pay expensive taxi fares to travel large distances on the islands, many vacationers will choose to rent a car for their touring of Trinidad. Sedans, jeeps, other four-wheel-drive vehicles, and even eight-passenger minivans can be rented from the various agencies on the island. Hertz and Thrifty are the only two international companies with offices on the island.

Review the following chart which identifies the various area vehicle rental agencies.

Trinidad

VEHICLE RENTAL COMPANIES

| Name | Phone | Location |
|---|---|---|
| A & A Car Rental | (868) 622-5588 | 37 Tragarete Road - Woodbrook |
| A-1 Auto Rentals | (868) 638-8125 | 66 Churchill Roosevelt Highway - The vicinity of Port of Spain |
| Alamo Morvant | (868) 675-7368 | Lady Young Road - 4.0 mi. (6.4 km) East of Port of Spain |
| Alamo POS | (868) 669-2277 | Piarco International Airport - 7.0 mi. (11.3 km) Northeast of Chaguanas |
| Alamo San Fernando | (868) 657-7368 | Gooding Village - San Fernando |
| Amar Rentals | (868) 622-6427 | 177 Tragarete Rd - Woodbrook |
| Auto Ram's Rental Ltd | (868) 771-4008 | Debe |
| Auto Rentals | (868) 675-7368 | Port of Spain |
| Autocenter Car Rentals | (868) 628-4400 | Woodbrook |
| Autopal Rental Services Ltd. | (868) 748-9620 | 10.8 mi. (17.4 km) Northeast of Chaguanas |
| Avis Piarco International | (868) 669- | Piarco International Airport - 7.0 mi. (11.3 km) |

| | | |
|---|---|---|
| Airport | 0905 | Northeast of Chaguanas |
| Avis Port of Spain | (868) 627-7753 | Crowne Plaza - Woodbrook |
| Bacchus Taxi & Car Rentals Co Ltd | (868) 622-5588 | Woodbrook |
| Basic Transport | (868) 624-0266 | Downtown Port of Spain |
| Big J Car Services | (868) 628-5701 | 70 Picton St Newtown - Downtown Port of Spain |
| Budget POS | (868) 669-1635 | Piarco International Airport - 7.0 mi. (11.3 km) Northeast of Chaguanas |
| Camel Transport Services | (868) 648-6438 | 51 Pt Fortin Main Rd Pt Fortin - Point Fortin |
| Car Limited | (868) 675-3245 | 10 Satar St Aranguez - Trinidad |
| Class Auto Rentals Services Ltd | (868) 652-1916 | 9 Perth Av - Trinidad |
| Convenient Rental Ltd | (868) 223-4017 | 5 Ranjit Kumar St - Downtown Port of Spain |
| Coral Cove Rentals | (868) 634-1034 | Western Main Road - Chaguaramas |
| Cupen's Garage | (868) 632-8736 | The vicinity of Port of Spain |

Trinidad

| | | |
|---|---|---|
| Den's Rental Service | (868) 657-3930 | San Fernando |
| Econ-Car Rentals Chaguaramas | (868) 634-2154 | Crews Inn Yacht Club - Chaguaramas |
| Econo-Car Rentals POS | (868) 669-1119 | Piarco International Airport - 7.0 mi. (11.3 km) Northeast of Chaguanas |
| Enterprise Rent A Car | (868) 800-8080 | The vicinity of Port of Spain |
| Europcar Trinidad & Tobago | (868) 621-2159 | Hilton Trinidad & Conference Centre - 3.3 mi. (5.3 km) East of Port of Spain |
| Exclusive Car Rentals | (868) 632-7812 | Chaguaramas |
| Executive Route Services Limited | (868) 653-4377 | 2-8 Riverside Dr SFDO - San Fernando |
| Furness Rentals Limited | (868) 627-4959 | Downtown Port of Spain |
| Hertz Golden Grove | (868) 669-6239 | Golden Grove Road - The vicinity of Port of Spain |
| High Quality Car Rentals | (868) 689-8757 | 11 Kalloo St - The vicinity of Port of Spain |
| Himraj Rental Service | (868) 800-3131 | Piarco International Airport - 7.0 mi. (11.3 km) Northeast of Chaguanas |
| Island Cars Trinidad Ltd | (868) 646- | D'abadie |

|  |  |  |
|---|---|---|
|  | 4746 |  |
| Kalloo's Auto Rentals | (868) 669-5673 | Piarco International Airport - 7.0 mi. (11.3 km) Northeast of Chaguanas |
| Kenny's Rentals | (868) 628-7129 | 6 Bournes Road - St. James |
| Lucas Car Rental | (868) 669-4131 | 8-10 Golden Grove Road - The vicinity of Port of Spain |
| Millenium Rentals | (868) 633-7363 | The vicinity of Port of Spain |
| Millennium Enterprises | (868) 627-1484 | 103-B St Vincent St POS - Downtown Port of Spain |
| Mini Shak Trading Co | (868) 640-1425 | Trincity Mall - The vicinity of Port of Spain |
| Nellex Rentals Co Ltd | (868) 677-7264 | Oropouche |
| Prince Motors Ltd | (868) 652-2795 | 23 Scott St SFdo - San Fernando |
| Ragoo's Auto Rental & Tyre Dealers | (868) 628-2756 | 53 Western Main Rd St James - St. James |
| Ramkissoon's Auto Rentals | (868) 679-2886 | Southern Main Rd Couva - Mac Bean |
| Rent-A-Car Ltd | (868) 657-9062 | San Fernando |

# Trinidad

| | | |
|---|---|---|
| Sav-A-Lot Rent A Car Ltd | (868) 669-2226 | Piarco International Airport - The vicinity of Port of Spain |
| Sigma Car Dealers Ltd | (868) 659-3452 | 9 Riley Road - Claxton Bay |
| Singh's Auto Rentals | (868) 623-0150 | 7-9 Wrightson Road - Port of Spain |
| Singh's Rentals POS | (868) 669-5417 | Piarco International Airport - 7.0 mi. (11.3 km) Northeast of Chaguanas |
| Singh's Rentals Sovonetta | (868) 636-7959 | Southern Main Road - California |
| Southern Executive Services Ltd | (868) 662-0884 | 60-B Spring Village - The vicinity of Port of Spain |
| Sue's Auto Rental | (868) 669-1635 | Golden Grove Road - The vicinity of Port of Spain |
| Supersad Auto Rentals Ltd | (868) 684-6711 | 123 Bejucal Road - Chaguanas |
| Swift Auto Rentals Ltd | (868) 648-7254 | Southern Main Road - La Brea |
| Thrifty Piarco International Airport | (868) 669-0602 | Piarco International Airport - 7.0 mi. (11.3 km) Northeast of Chaguanas |
| Tri Star Auto Rental's | (868) 767-9797 | Cor Kalloo Street & Southern Main Road - The vicinity of Port of Spain |
| Triple D'S Equipment | (868) 800- | Southern Main Road - Gran Couva |

|  |  |  |
|---|---|---|
| Rentals Ltd | 4333 |  |
| United Caribbean Services Ltd | (868) 627-7753 | Crowne Plaza - Port of Spain |
| Vehicle Leasing & Rental Estate Limited | (868) 800-0672 | 6 Queen Street - The vicinity of Port of Spain |
| Xtra Lease & Rental Company Ltd | (868) 355-0812 | 1B Marajh Drive - Chaguanas |

## The Cost of Renting a Car

Rates can start as low as $35(USD) and go up to $70(USD) for more expensive vehicles. Some of the large passenger vans will exceed $100(USD).

This set of tables provide a general indication of what sort of rate you will pay. The lowest rates shown are usually only available from the least expensive agencies during the slowest times of the year. The highest rates are what you might need to pay during the peak season.

| VEHICLE RENTALS, DAILY RATES | | |
|---|---|---|
| Rental Type | Low Rate | High Rate |
| Economy Car | $ 37.50 | $ 75.00 |
| Mid Size Car | $ 50.00 | $ 90.00 |

## Trinidad

| Rental Type | Low Rate | High Rate |
|---|---|---|
| Compact Car | $ 58.00 | $ 81.00 |
| Standard SUV | $ 75.00 | $ 121.00 |
| Light SUV | $ 82.00 | $ 135.00 |
| Mini Van | $ 85.00 | $ 152.00 |
| Full Size Car | $ 90.00 | $ 125.00 |

VEHICLE RENTALS, WEEKLY RATES

| Rental Type | Low Rate | High Rate |
|---|---|---|
| Economy Car | $ 225.00 | $ 487.50 |
| Mid Size Car | $ 295.00 | $ 585.00 |
| Compact Car | $ 345.00 | $ 498.00 |
| Standard SUV | $ 450.00 | $ 730.00 |
| Light SUV | $ 492.00 | $ 878.00 |
| Mini Van | $ 510.00 | $ 988.00 |
| Full Size Car | $ 540.00 | $ 812.00 |

Drivers who wish to rent a car on Trinidad will need an international driver's permit or a valid license issued in The Bahamas, Canada, England, France, Germany, or the United States. These licenses are valid for 90 days while staying on the islands. Drivers are generally required to be 25 years old and have had at least two years of driving experience. A major credit card is also required. Gas is not included in the price, and travelers are generally given unlimited mileage. Collision damage insurance is highly recommended, and travelers can usually secure this type of insurance for $10(USD) to $20(USD) per day. Varying daily rates will reduce your liability to $500(USD) or to no liability. Be sure to review all policies, rates, and insurance agreements with the local car rental firms.

Be sure to call and ask about any other requirements.

## Driving on Trinidad

Drivers on Trinidad, a former British colony, stay to the left-hand side of the road. Travelers from North America and Europe will need to drive cautiously to adjust to this change. Drivers and passengers in the front seat are required by law to wear seatbelts. Some of the usual hazards that plague driving conditions in the Caribbean exist, including roads that are not well maintained and animal and pedestrian traffic. Nighttime driving is not recommended because of road conditions and intoxicated drivers. Local drivers may use hand signals that are unfamiliar to international drivers to indicate turns or stops. Visiting drivers should drive defensively and cautiously to avoid getting into trouble in their rental car on either island.

Be sure to check the listing below which presents various refueling options in and around Trinidad.

## GAS STATIONS

| Name | Location |
| --- | --- |
| Cantaro Gas Station | Saddle Road - 5.9 mi. (9.6 km) Northeast of Port of Spain |
| NP Aranguez | Aranguez Main Road and Backchain Street - San Juan |
| NP Audrey Jeffers | Audrey Jeffers Highway and Mucurapo Road - 1.0 mi. (1.6 km) North-Northwest of Port of Spain |
| NP Beetham Highway | Beetham Highway - 3.4 mi. (5.5 km) East of Port of Spain |
| NP Cunupia | Southern Main Road and Chin Chin Road - 3.2 mi. (5.2 km) Northeast of Chaguanas |
| NP Diego Martin | St. Lucien Road - 3.9 mi. (6.3 km) North-Northwest of Port of Spain |
| NP Fifth Street | Fifth Street and Eight Avenue - San Juan |
| NP Gas UWI | Eastern Main Road next to University of the West Indies - St. Augustine |
| NP Lady Young | Lady Young and Eastern Main Roads - San Juan |
| NP Maraval | Saddle Road - Maraval |
| NP Maraval Road | Maraval and Tragarete Roads - Woodbrook |
| NP Morne Coco | Morne Coco Road and Diego Martin Main Road - 2.3 mi. (3.8 km) Northwest of Port of Spain |

| | |
|---|---|
| NP Mt. Hope | Eastern Main Road and Maloney Street - San Juan |
| NP Old Southern Road | Intersection of Old Southern Road and Southern Road - Montrose |
| NP Park Street | Park Street and Richmond Street - 1.5 mi. (2.4 km) East of Port of Spain |
| NP Piarco | B.W.I.A Boulevard - 7.4 mi. (11.9 km) Northeast of Chaguanas |
| NP Pierre Road | Pierre Road and Caroni Savannah Road - 1.4 mi. (2.2 km) North of Chaguanas |
| NP Tenth Street | Tenth Street - San Juan |
| NP Tragarete Road | Tragarete Road and Richmond Street - 1.5 mi. (2.4 km) East of Port of Spain |
| NP Wrightson Road | Wrightson Road and Gatacre Street - Woodbrook |
| Peakes One Stop Service Station | 1.2 mi. (2.0 km) North-Northwest of Port of Spain |
| Unipet Gas | Eastern Main Road by Orange Grove Road - 8.6 mi. (13.9 km) North-Northeast of Chaguanas |
| Unipet Medford | Edinburg Boulevard Roundabout at Sir Solomon Highway - Montrose |

# Sailing & Boating

## Sailing and Boating Near Trinidad

## Sailing and yachting are fun activities while on vacation

Geography and location have made the waters surrounding Trinidad and Tobago popular sailing and yachting spots for vacationers seeking fun on the sea. Most insurance companies require boats to spend the hurricane season in locations south of latitude 12 degrees. Trinidad and Tobago are located at latitude 10.5 and 11 degrees North, so while in their waters, boaters usually don't have to worry about their insurance.

## Boat Trips and Day Sailing

Before we discuss the various options for sailors or those looking for charters, there are options for the average tourists looking for a fun activity without much of a hassle. For these visitors, day sails and excursions are the way to go. These trips are usually preplanned and sold as packages by the company, and all you do is go along for the ride. Trips can be centered on activities (like diving or beach hopping) or focused on visiting different locations.

If you're just wanting to get out onto the water, without the cost and complications of sailing on your own you should take a day sailing excursion. See the listing below for names and phone numbers for area excursion providers.

BOAT EXCURSIONS

| Name | Phone | Location |
|---|---|---|
| Kelvin Cruise & Travel Service | (868) 659-0271 | Claxton Bay |
| T J's Island Cruises | (868) 653-0408 | South Trunk Road - Trinidad |
| Trinidad Charters | (868) 771-2461 | Coral Cove Marina - Chaguaramas |

## Boat Rentals and Charters

Charter brokers can help you make many important decisions about your charter, including finding the right crew for your trip. Charter brokers represent the owner of the yacht and help find both crewed and bareboat charters. Having a crew that fits your needs is important to the enjoyment of your charter. You will want to have a crew that is both knowledgeable and with personalities that fit your style. Charter brokers are available at no extra cost because they are paid by the charter companies.

If you're serious about renting a boat, you can reserve one from the following agencies:

| CHARTER AND RENTAL SERVICES | | |
|---|---|---|
| Name | Phone | Location |
| Boyceterous 30ft Catmaran | (868) 680-9888 | Chaguaramas |

## Trinidad

| | | |
|---|---|---|
| Calypso Marine Services | (868) 634-4551 | Western Main Rd Chag - Chaguaramas |
| I M S Yacht Services | (868) 625-2104 | First Avenue - Chaguanas |
| Oceanfreight Trinidad Ltd | (868) 625-3835 | Woodbrook |
| Pier 1 | (868) 634-4472 | Pier 1 Marina - 5.2 mi. (8.4 km) West-Northwest of Port of Spain |
| South Caribbean Charters Ltd | (868) 678-1426 | 43 Beechwood Drive - The vicinity of Port of Spain |

There are two types of charter companies you will be able to choose from when getting a charter boat: large and small. The larger charter companies provide more guarantees than the smaller one. If this is you first charter, you should probably work with a larger company in case the boat you originally wanted is not available. Unlike a small company, a large company will be able to provide a boat that is almost the same if not larger at no extra cost. If you're not sure about what kind of charter is right for you or you have questions about a particular charter company, a charter broker can assist you in finding the right charter for you.

Another way to choose a charter company is by tier. There are two tiers of charter companies. First tier charter companies have the newest boats, which are stocked with the most current and up-to-date equipment and technology. The boats found at first tier companies are about 4 to 5 years old or younger and have only been used by that first tier company. Second tier companies often acquire their boats from the fleets of first tier companies. The ships at second tier companies are usually more affordable than first tiers, but they may not have all the technological extras like CD players and cellular phones.

**Docking**

With recent improvements in docking facilities, sailing and yachting marinas have become some of the best places for boating in the Eastern Caribbean. Seamen are attracted to the island because of its safe harbors and the area's location outside the hurricane belt. The main ports on Trinidad are Chaguanas and the Port of Spain, a commercial port where yachters only stop during times of emergency. The main ports on Tobago are Charlottesville and Scarborough.

To dock at these ports, boaters must go through some basic clearance requirements. On Trinidad, sailors should land on port Chaguaramas, where entry formalities can be completed. Boaters are required to present a clearance-out certificate from the last port they visited when docking in Chaguaramas. For any questions or marina information on Trinidad, boaters can call the customs office at 868-634-4341 or contact immigration at 868-634-4341 on the island. On Tobago, sailboats and yachts can gain clearance at the Charlottesville port, which has protected anchorage.

Are you going to sail to Trinidad in your own vessel, or a charter from another location? The following chart provides a quick summary of nearby marinas.

MARINAS

| Name | Phone | Location |
| --- | --- | --- |
| Coral Cove Marina | (868) 634-2040 | Western Main Road - Chaguaramas |
| Crews Inn Marina | (868) 634-4384 | Crews Inn - Chaguaramas |
| Ims Yacht Services | -- | Chaguaramas |
| Pier 1 Marina | (868) 634-4472 | Dale Ramsumair - |
| Power Boat Mutual Facilities Ltd | (868) 634-4303 | Chaguaramas |
| Power Boat Mutual Facilities Ltd | (868) 634-4303 | Chaguaramas |

| | | |
|---|---|---|
| San Fernando Yacht Club | (868) 652-3937 | Hubert Rance Street - San Fernando |
| Sweetwater Marina Ltd (The Lure) | (868) 634-2773 | 2 Stella Maris Drive - Chaguanas |
| Tardieu Marine Ltd | (868) 634-4534 | 110 Western Main Road - Port of Spain |
| The Marina in Chaguanas | (868) 634-4183 | Point Gourge - Chaguanas |
| Trinidad & Tobago Yacht Club | (868) 633-7420 | Bayshore Point - Port of Spain |
| Tropical Marine | (868) 634-4502 | Western Main Road - Chaguanas |

Both Trinidad and Tobago hold annual boating events and regattas, which are popular among vacationers. One of the most exciting and popular events is Carnival, during which vacationers may spend weeks exploring the waters off the shores of Trinidad and Tobago. Many travelers charter yachts and sailboats for water excursions, and the waters tend to get somewhat crowded during this time of year, so be sure to make any necessary boating arrangements before your vacation. For any questions and information on sailing and yachting on the islands, boaters can contact the Trinidad and Tobago Sailing

Association at P.O. Box 3140, Carenage Post Office, Trinidad West Indies, or by phone at 868-634-4210 or 868-634-4519 on the island.

NEARBY ANCHORAGES

| Location | Latitude | Longitude |
|---|---|---|
| Carenage Bay - 6.0 mi. (9.6 km) West of Port of Spain | 10.6809676743 | -61.6207695007 |
| Chaguaramas | 10.6791381679 | -61.6345882416 |

Chartering a yacht or sailing yourself is a great way to explore the waters of Trinidad and Tobago.

# Taxis on Trinidad

Taxis are a hassle-free way to travel while vacationing on Trinidad and Tobago

Vacationers who want a quick and easy way to get around Trinidad can hail one of the island's taxi cabs, which can be found almost anywhere on the island.

## Taxi Companies

Taxis usually meet most flights at Piarco International Airport, and can also be found near hotels and other attractions. While your resort concierge will typically be happy to help you call a cab, if you're out an about and need to hail a cab on your own, you'll quickly know that you've found a valid driver by the letter "H" on his license plate, and by his uniform. Taxi drivers on Trinidad and Tobago werar white shirt jackets, black or blue pants, and have a yellow identification pass. If one of these things is missing, leave the vehicle immediately and find a different driver to avoid being swindled.

Take a look at the listing below to find contact phone numbers for local cab companies.

| TAXI SERVICES | | |
| --- | --- | --- |
| Name | Phone | Location |
| 800 Taxi | (868) 697-0517 | 3 Canaan Rd La Romain - San Fernando |
| A & A Taxi | (868) 622-5588 | 37 Tragarete Road - Woodbrook |
| A-1 Taxi Service | (868) 638-8125 | 66 Churchill Roosevelt Highway - The vicinity of Port of Spain |
| Amc Taxi Transport & Courier Services | (868) 658-4973 | 68 Sea View Dr - The vicinity of Port of Spain |
| Broadway Taxi Service | (868) 623-7304 | Independence Square - Port of Spain |
| Caribbean Limo & Cab Services | (868) 640-0040 | 24 Hour Service - Trinidad |

Trinidad

| Name | Phone | Address |
|---|---|---|
| Executive Consolidated Taxi Service | (868) 630-8123 | Vicks Avenue - Mayaro |
| Himraj Taxi | (868) 800-3131 | Piarco International Airport - 7.0 mi. (11.3 km) Northeast of Chaguanas |
| Ice House Taxi Service | (868) 627-6984 | Abercromby Street - Port of Spain |
| Kalloos Taxi Service & Tours | (868) 669-5673 | Piarco International Airport - 7.0 mi. (11.3 km) Northeast of Chaguanas |
| Kapok Taxi Service | (868) 622-6995 | 16-18 Cotton Hill - St. Clair |
| Lucas Taxi Service | (868) 669-4131 | 8-10 Golden Grove Road - The vicinity of Port of Spain |
| Mattadeen's Taxi-Cab Service | (868) 658-4973 | 68 Sea View Dr Marabella - San Fernando |
| Mike's Taxi Car Rental & 24 Hr Wrecker Service | (868) 624-1522 | 37 Industry Lane - The vicinity of Port of Spain |
| Phone A Taxi | (868) 628-8294 | Trinidad |
| Route 2 Maxi Taxi Association | (868) 624-3505 | South Quay - Port of Spain |
| Southern Tax Services | (868) 697-0521 | 319 Southern Main Road - Trinidad |
| St Anthony's Taxi Cab Co- | (868) 648- | Point Fortin |

| | | |
|---|---|---|
| Operative | 3941 | |
| Suncoast Enterprises Ltd | (868) 647-0719 | Penal |
| Taxi Service | (868) 669-0282 | 12 Roedler Road - Trinidad |
| Transport Solutions Ltd | (868) 669-4332 | 17 St Helena Village - The vicinity of Port of Spain |
| Transport Specialists Limited | (868) 800-0672 | 6 Queen Street, St. Joseph - The vicinity of Port of Spain |
| Trinidad & Tobago Tourist Transport Services Association | (868) 623-4419 | Cruise Ship Complex - 1.3 mi. (2.2 km) East-Southeast of Port of Spain |
| William's Call Taxi Service | (868) 657-7408 | 10A Princess Street - San Fernando |
| Yellow Cab Services | (868) 645-8294 | 1 College Road - St. Augustine |

## Rates, Fares, and Fees

The main concern of most taxi companies is the comfort of their passengers, and some cabs even have left-hand-drive cars to make their customers feel more like they are riding at home. When hailing a cab, remember that fares are not regulated by the government, and most cabs have fixed rates according to the distance of the trip.

Usually cab fare is inexpensive, but travelers should make sure to negotiate the cost of your trip with the driver before you set off for your destination. The airports usually post cab fares in U.S. and TT dollars.

This chart provides some taxi rates for this area.

TYPICAL FARES AROUND TRINIDAD

| Typical Cost (USD) | Location A | Location B |
|---|---|---|
| $ 23.00 - $ 40.00 | Piarco International Airport | San Juan |
| $ 55.00 - $ 85.00 | Piarco International Airport | Princes Town |
| $ 45.00 - $ 70.00 | Piarco International Airport | Chaguaramas |
| $ 110.00 - $ 170.00 | Piarco International Airport | Icacos |
| $ 80.00 - $ 125.00 | Piarco International Airport | Point Fortin |
| $ 40.00 - $ 65.00 | Piarco International Airport | Gran Couva |
| $ 30.00 - $ 50.00 | Piarco International Airport | Downtown Port Of Spain |
| $ 50.00 - $ 80.00 | Piarco International Airport | San Fernando |
| $ 20.00 - $ 35.00 | Piarco International Airport | Arima |
| $ 35.00 - $ 60.00 | Piarco International Airport | Sangre Grande |

Travelers will have to pay a 50 percent surcharge when catching a cab on Trinidad and Tobago between the hours of 10:00 p.m. and 6:00 a.m. and drivers reserve the right to charge extra for use of the trunk.

**Additional Information**

From busy city streets to empy country lanes, driving on Trinidad can vary. Because of this, so can the process of getting a cab. To learn the specifics of local areas, read one of our guides below.

| TAXI SERVICES IN SPECIFIC AREAS |
| --- |
| Guide to Chaguanas Taxis |
| Guide to Port of Spain Taxis |
| Guide to Tobago Taxis |

While they can be expensive, hiring a cab to drive you from place to place allows you to sit back and enjoy the ride, taking in the sites as you go back and savoring every moment.

# Travel Basics

Travel Fundamentals for Trinidad
**Vacationers will find friendly people and distinct regions on Trinidad and Tobago**

Learning local etiquette and some basic background information on the different regions of Trinidad and Tobago will help you plan a trip that caters to your interests. From bustling capital cities to pristine quiet beaches, it's good to know where to go and how to be respectful once you get there.

**Etiquette**

There is no better way for travelers to endear themselves to locals than to demonstrate a knowledge of and respect for local customs and etiquette. When you travel abroad, you are in someone else's home. Travelers should always be courteous and use common sense when visiting all areas of Trinidad and Tobago. Always dispose of your garbage in trash receptacles. Avoid using inappropriate language in public. Travelers should heed this warning especially because public use of inappropriate language on Trinidad and Tobago is punishable with arrest and fines.

When surrounded by unique people, many visitors to Trinidad and Tobago take lots of pictures. Photos are great mementos, but you should always ask permission before aiming your lens at a resident on Trinidad and Tobago. Asking before you snap the photo is a small gesture but helps avoid any misunderstandings.

Local service staff, whether in a restaurant, hotel, or taxi, should be tipped according to local customs. Business travelers should always shake hands and exchange business cards upon introduction.

Visitors should also be aware that their beach and revealing clothing is not considered appropriate attire anywhere but the beach. Swimsuits, shorts, bikini tops, and flip flops should not be worn in restaurants, shops, public hotel areas, and cities.

Travelers can also make themselves aware of local expressions that may be used during their travels. To "lime," for example, is to hang out and party. This expression could be the most important! Formalities such as "good morning" should also be used when greeting someone.

Travelers who are conscious of local customs and standards for behavior on Trinidad and Tobago are sure to be appreciated by locals.

## Regions on Trinidad

### Port of Spain

Port of Spain, is the capital of Trinidad, the active hub of the island both culturally and economically. The city boasts a zoo and museum, and visitors can enjoy shopping for local crafts. Hotels and nightlife on the island are largely in Port of Spain. Carnival in Port of Spain is a unique occasion full of revelry, costume, and dance.

## Chaguaramas

Encompassing the area and islands west of Port of Spain, the area of Chaguaramas is perhaps best known to yachters and nature enthusiasts. Over 14,000 acres of largely unspoiled and varied terrain, the region offers a large national park, ecoadventure, beaches, and a popular marina for yachters.

## Northeast

Another undeveloped and unspoiled area, the Northeast part of the island, including Toco and Matelot offers travelers a hideaway on the island. Beaches, rainforests, and a sparse population cater to travelers looking to get away, but amenities and services in this area are not common.

## The North and Blanchisseuse

Blanchisseuse is a small fishing village that plays host to travelers looking to enjoy the beauty and quiet of the surrounding ocean and forest terrain. Waters can be rough, but the unspoiled rainforests offer travelers other natural diversions. Several other beach areas can be found in this area, including Las Cuevas and Maracas Bay. The Asa Wright Nature Centre has a cornucopia of bird species for bird lovers.

## The South and The East

The southern and eastern parts of the island are both largely undeveloped. The east coast of the island has two attractive beaches, Manzanilla and Mayaro. The south part of the island is home to San Fernando (the island's other major city) and the oil industry, but this area remains largely unspoiled and unpopulated. Travelers will not find the tourist amenities of restaurants and hotels in abundance.

## Regions on Tobago

### Scarborough

The capital of Tobago does not attract large droves of tourists, but does have markets, museums, and gardens. Bacolet, to the east, offers travelers restaurants, beaches, and hotels.

### Crown Point

Crown Point is home to the airport on Tobago, and beaches such as Store Bay and Pigeon Point often give air travelers reason to stay in the area. Restaurants, accommodations, and nightlife are also available in Crown Point, as well as in Buccoo to the northeast.

### Northeast

This area has the villages of Speyside and Charlotteville, both of which are largely off the radar. This is a popular area for divers, but the rough waters make swimming in the area treacherous. Both locations have a number of small and quaint accommodations.

**North Coast**

This is a largely undeveloped area on the island full of nature preserves, beaches, and quiet seaside villages such as Castara and Parlatuvier

Trinidad and Tobago offer travelers from all over the world prime opportunities to escape crowds by enjoying unspoiled and quiet natural environments. At the same time, travelers looking for culture and activity can find it in Port of Spain and in the Crown Point area of Tobago. Travelers in any region of Trinidad and Tobago should make good use of etiquette and courtesy to endear themselves to friendly residents.

# Clothing

## Clothing and Attire on Trinidad
**Attire on Trinidad and Tobago is similar to much of the Caribbean**
Trinidad and Tobago are closer to the equator than other Caribbean destinations, which results in hot, humid conditions. Visitors will want to pack appropriate items to stay cool while conforming to local customs for dress.

Weather on Trinidad and Tobago is generally pleasant, with an average yearly temperature of 82 degrees Fahrenheit. Temperatures can fluctuate, with cool evenings and hot and humid days driving temperatures up or down from the average. In order to stay cool during warm days, pack clothes made from light fabrics that allow ventilation. Clothing made of linen and cotton are the best choices. Travelers may want to avoid packing snug, tight-fitting clothing because of the heat. Clothing should be relaxed and casual, but neat. A sweater or light jacket comes in handy during winter evenings, or when visiting the region's higher altitudes.

Trinidad and Tobago's rainy season lasts from June to December, and if you visit the islands during these months, definitely pack protective rain gear in case you are caught in a typical afternoon shower.

Be sure to pack plenty of beach and active wear clothing, including swimsuits, athletic shorts and shoes, sandals, hats, sunglasses, tank tops, and shorts. Travelers who know they will be enjoying a recreational activity such as mountain biking will want to pack the necessary equipment for their excursion. Hats, sunglasses, and sunscreen provide protection from the powerful sun. Beachwear, activewear, shorts, and other revealing pieces of clothing should not be worn in cities, shops, restaurants, or in hotel lobbies. When out, men should wear pants and a collared or button down shirt. Women can wear informal dresses.

While most vacationers will not need to bring formal wear, travelers should be sure to consider their itinerary when packing. Pack accordingly if a business meeting or upscale dinner requires a tie, jacket, or even a suit.

Most visitors to the the Caribbean want to relax in comfortable clothing while enjoying the tropical weather and exploring the culture and beauty of the islands. Luckily, for travelers to Trinidad and Tobago, dress codes are laid back, and packing should be light and simple.

# Currency

## Trinidad's currency options
**Travelers should exchange their cash once they land on the islands**
Paying for services, accommodations, and dining is easy on Trinidad and Tobago. Even though the islands use their own currency, credit cards are widely accepted.

For cash, you will need Trinidad and Tobago dollars (TT$). Trinidad and Tobago coins are issued in denominations of TT$0.01, TT$0.05, TT$0.10, TT$0.25, and TT$0.50. Coins are engraved with the islands' coat of arms on one side and one of the national birds or flowers on the other. Trinidad and Tobago notes are issued in denominations of TT$1, TT$5, TT$10, TT$20, and TT$100. At the time of writing, the exchange rate to several major international currencies was TT$6.26

to $1.00(USD); TT$7.64 to ?1.00; and TT$11.25 to £1.00. Merchants usually accept U.S. dollars, but travelers are generally advised to change their money once they reach the island. Banks and currency exchange bureaus throughout Port of Spain and in the airport allow travelers to change their currency into Trinidad and Tobago dollars.

Major credit cards are widely accepted at many types of establishments throughout Trinidad and Tobago, and this should help prevent travelers from exchanging large sums of hard currency to finance your stay. Visa and Mastercard are more widely accepted than American Express and other credit cards. Travelers checks are also accepted throughout the islands, though travelers should always have cash handy to pay small vendors, taxi and bus fares, and tips.

Banks on the island include the First Citizen Bank, Scotiabank, The Republic Bank, and The Royal Bank of Trinidad and Tobago (RBTT). ATMs accepting cards on the Plus/Electron and Cirrus/Maestro networks are available. Visitors to the island will find ATMs in both the Piarco International Airport on Trinidad and the Crown Point International Airport on Tobago. ATMs are also available throughout Port of Spain and Scarborough, but become harder to find outside the two major cities.

Although no one enjoys paying bills, wide acceptance of cash, credit cards, and traveler's checks makes it easy to pay your way through a Trinidad and Tobago vacation.

# Customs

## Getting Through Customs on Trinidad

**Going through customs is made easier by knowing the policy on regulated and restricted goods**

Everyone has things they can't live without during a vacation, and travel officials expect a certain amount of personal items to be brought into Trinidad and Tobago when visitors arrive. You'll likely be carrying out more items on the trip home than you came in with, so it's important to anticipate any taxes or restrictions on items brought into and taken out of Trinidad and Tobago.

When arriving on Trinidad and Tobago, all visitors must pass through immigration and customs, where luggage and personal property may be inspected. To avoid possible delays or even pricey taxation on items you are traveling with, you should know Trinidad and Tobago's customs policies as well as those of your home country. Sometimes customs lines are long and delays inevitable, but most can gain clearance through customs with relative ease when you know what to expect.

Several items must be declared before you may gain clearance through both islands' customs. Tobacco and alcohol products are regulated when visiting most islands in the Caribbean, so travelers are permitted to bring up to 200 cigarettes or 50 cigars and up to 1 quart of liquor or spirits without any taxation or duty when entering Trinidad and Tobago. Other personal items such as clothing and most electronics can be brought to the island duty-free.

When packing for your vacation, try to bring only the necessary personal items. If you bring an excessive amount of personal items, customs officers may impose a charge on them if they believe these items exceed the quantity for personal use. These items are either prohibited or regulated when visiting Trinidad or Tobago:

- Weapons and firearms are not allowed to be shipped or brought onto the island.
- Narcotics and illegal drugs cannot be brought to Trinidad or Tobago, and vacationers must have all of their prescription drugs in originally labeled bottles. Prescription drugs are not allowed to be shipped to the island.
- Food and plant products are regulated and often restricted when entering the country, and some animals including dogs

and cats are prohibited from visiting the islands, unless they meet certain requirements.

Travelers can find more information about restricted and prohibited items by contacting any of these agencies:

| Agency | Contact Info |
|---|---|
| Customs and Excise Division | Nicholas Court<br>Abercromby Street & Independence Square<br>Port-of-Spain, Trinidad<br>868-625-3311 |
| Trinidad and Tobago Bureau of Standards | Lot 1, Century Drive<br>Trincity Industrial Estate<br>Macoya<br>868-662-8827 |
| Ministry of Health | Chemistry/Food and Drugs Division<br>92 Frederick Street<br>Port-of-Spain<br>868-623-2834 |
| Ministry of Food Production and Resources | Plant Quarantine<br>Port Marine Building<br>Queen's Wharf<br>Port-of-Spain<br>868-625-3266 |

Travelers returning to the United States will also have to be aware that some items could be taxed or prohibited. Most items must fall under certain quantities to enter without penalty. These are the items that are regulated by U.S. customs and the amounts in which they can be brought into the country:

If you're 21 or older, vacationers can bring up to one liter of alcohol into the country. Up to one liter of perfume containing alcohol can be brought back into the country as well as 200 cigarettes and 100 non-Cuban cigars.

Packages can be sent home without duty as long as it is one parcel per addressee per day, with the exception of alcohol and tobacco products, or perfume worth more than $5(USD).

Original works of art including sculptures and painting and antiques (objects more than 100 years old) can be brought into the country duty-free.

Up to $200(USD) in goods can be mailed to the United States as long as they are for personal use. Vacationers should be sure to mark "PERSONAL USE" on the outside of the parcel and attach a list of its contents and their retail value.

When sending a parcel containing goods that have been used, mark the parcel "AMERICAN GOODS RETURNED" to avoid duty charges.

Customs policies are subject to change, but travelers can keep up to date with the most current information by checking with their home countries' customs. This list contains contact information for some customs offices around the world:

| Country | Contact |
| --- | --- |
| United States | U.S. Customs Service<br>1300 Pennsylvania Ave., NW<br>Washington, DC 20229<br>877-227-5511<br>http://www.cbp.gov |
| United Kingdom | HM Customs & Excise<br>0845-010-9000<br>http://www.hmrc.gov.uk/index.htm |
| Canada | Canada Customs and Revenue Agency<br>800-461-9999<br>www.ccra-adrc.gc.ca |
| Australia | Australian Customs Service<br>1300-363-263<br>www.customs.gov.au |
| New Zeland | New Zealand Customs Service<br>04-473-6099 |

www.customs.govt.nz

By understanding the customs policies of Trinidad and Tobago as well as the requirements of their home country, travelers can pass through customs more smoothly and be on their way to enjoying their tropical island getaway.

# Driving

## Roadway Guidance on Trinidad

**Drivers should be cautious of left-hand driving and Caribbean road conditions**

Road conditions, driving customs, and driving behaviors can be vastly different from what you're used to, especially in the Caribbean, where roads and drivers can be somewhat unpredictable. Although Trinidad and Tobago achieved independence from England in 1962, drivers stay to the left-hand side of the road on both islands.

If you're traveling from North American or mainland Europe, take time to adjust to the change in direction and be cautious when you take the wheel. International visitors to Trinidad and Tobago may drive on the islands for up to 90 days but must have an International Driver's Permit or a valid driver's license from the Bahamas, Canada, England, France, Germany, or the United States. Most rental car companies require drivers to be at least 25 years old and have two years of driving experience. Front-seat passengers and drivers are required by law to wear seatbelts. Gas stations are located throughout Trinidad but are generally harder to find on Tobago.

Many main roads on Trinidad and Tobago are in good condition, and several well-maintained highways accommodate automobile traffic on Trinidad. Drivers in Port of Spain should be aware of aggressive drivers and gridlocked rush hours. Other roads on Trinidad and Tobago may suffer from typical Caribbean problems. Roads can be thin and curving and can also be flanked by steep embankments that make driving off the road doubly dangerous. Night-time driving is not generally recommended for international visitors because intoxicated drivers are common on both islands. Drivers should always be aware of animals and pedestrians that may cross into the road, and should take extra caution when taking blind corners. Local drivers can use hand signals that are unfamiliar to visitors from foreign countries to indicate turns and stops.

Trinidad makes it easy for tourists to avoid driving all together with their reliable and friendly bus service. The color coding on the buses makes them easy to use, even for long trips, and they are affordable to boot. Hailing a cab is another reliable means of getting around, though the price will be slightly higher than a bus ride.

Many visitors to Trinidad and Tobago enjoy the freedom of renting a car. Whether you set off to see the yachting area of Chaguaramas or the birds in the Asa Wright Nature Centre, exercise caution when taking to the road.

# Electricity

## Outlets and Voltage on Trinidad
**Vacationers may need to adapt to the islands' voltages**
For many vacationers, it's hard to do without important electrical items, such as hair dryers, irons, laptops, and other devices that make everyday life comfortable and easy. When booking hotel or resort arrangements for your stay on Trinidad and Tobago, be sure to inquire about the electricity and whether you will need to purchase an adapter or transformer.

Trinidad and Tobago has both 115 or 230-volt AC on 60 cycles. You should find out what voltage your hotel or resort uses before you go because these voltages may be different from your home country.

If your hotel's voltage does not match your appliances, you may need to purchase an adapter or transformer before you go or ask if one will be available to you once you check in. Some hotels often will offer their guests these items as part of their service. Some hotels may even have 220-volt outlets, which is what you find in most places in North America. Also, airports will probably carry the necessary equipment for converting your electrical appliances for use on the island.

You should easily be able to use all your personal electrical appliances on Trinidad and Tobago. Just be sure to talk to your hotel's staff about voltage requirements before you go and arrive prepared with the right equipment.

## Embassies

### Foreign Outposts on Trinidad
Embassies and consulates can provide help to travelers in foreign countries

Foreign countries can be lonely places if you encounter trouble during your travels. Whether you are the victim of a crime or you become trapped by a natural disaster or civil unrest, your local embassy and consulate can provide assistance. Visitors to Trinidad and Tobago should have the contact information for their local embassy or consulate in case assistance from a home country is required.

Travelers on the islands who fall victim to a crime should contact the local law enforcement authorities as well as their local embassy or consulate. Agents of the embassy or consulate can help secure medical or financial aid that may be needed as a result of the crime. If you are imprisoned on Trinidad and Tobago, always contact your local embassy or consular agent. While representatives and agents from your embassy do not act as lawyers, they can help you obtain legal representation and educate you about the judicial system on Trinidad and Tobago. They will also monitor your condition to ensure humane treatment and nutrition, and they can be in contact with authorities and relatives who are either on the islands or back in your home country.

Hurricanes, earthquakes, flooding, and mudslides can all be issues on Trinidad and Tobago, and citizens who are caught in the country during these times should contact their local embassy or consulate for advice. Purchasing travel insurance from travel agents can help cover the expense of an emergency trip out of the country. Travelers should also seek assistance of their local representatives in times of civil unrest.

The Bureau of Consular Affairs in the United States provides an article on tips for safe travel abroad. Travelers from the United States to foreign countries should also register their trip abroad through the State Department. This allows the State Department to have a list of the names of citizens traveling in a country if a natural disaster or other emergency may occur.

## Foreign embassies on Trinidad and Tobago:

| Embassy / Consulate | Contact Information |
|---|---|
| United States Embassy | 15 Queen's Park West<br>Port of Spain, Trinidad<br>868-622-6371<br>868-628-5462 (Fax)<br>http://trinidad.usembassy.gov/<br><br>American Citizens Services:<br>868-622-6371<br>868-628-9036 (Fax)<br>ACSPOS@state.gov<br><br>Hours:<br>Monday - Friday 7:30 a.m. - 4:30 p.m. |
| British High Commission | 19 St Clair Avenue<br>St Clair<br>Port of Spain, Trinidad<br>868-622-2748<br>868-622-4555 (Fax)<br>868-662-3377 (Emergency)<br>http://www.fco.gov.uk<br>E-mail: csbhc@tstt.net.tt |

| | |
|---|---|
| | Hours: |
| | Monday - Thursday 7:30 a.m. - 12:00 p.m., 1:00 p.m. - 4:00 p.m. |
| | Friday 7:30 a.m. - 12:30 p.m. |
| Canadian High Commission | Maple House, 3-3A |
| | Sweet Briar Rd., St. Clair |
| | Port of Spain, Trinidad |
| | 868-622-6232 |
| | 868-628-1830 (Fax) |
| | 800-387-3124 (Emergency) |
| | |
| | Mailing Address: |
| | The High Commission for Canada |
| | P.O. Box 1246 |
| | Port of Spain |
| | Republic of Trinidad and Tobago |
| | http://www.dfait-maeci.gc.ca/trinidadtobago/menu-en.asp |
| | E-mail: pspan@international.gc.ca |
| | |
| | Hours: |
| | Monday - Thursday 7:30 a.m. - 4:00 p.m. |
| | Friday 7:30 a.m. - 1:00 p.m. |
| Australian High Commission | 18 Herbert Street |
| | St Clair |
| | Port of Spain |
| | 868-628-4732 |
| | 868-622-0659 (Fax) |

Trinidad

http://www.trinidadandtobago.embassy.gov.au/

| | |
|---|---|
| New Zealand High Commission - Ottawa, Canada | Metropolitan House, Suite 727<br>99 Bank Street<br>Ottawa, Canada K1P 6G3<br>613-238-5991<br>613-238-5707 (Fax)<br>http://www.nzembassy.com/home.cfm?c=38<br>E-mail: info@nzhcottawa.org |
| Royal Netherlands Embassy | PO Box 870<br>69-71 Edward Street<br>Port of Spain, Trinidad<br>868-625-1210<br>http://trinidadandtobago.nlembassy.org/ |
| Embassy of France | Tatil Building<br>11 Maraval Road<br>PO Box 1242<br>Port of Spain, Trinidad<br>868-622-7446<br>868-628-2632 (Fax)<br>http://www.ambafrance-tt.org/spip.php?rubrique2 |
| German Embassy | 7-9 Marli Street Newtown<br>P.O. Box 828<br>Port of Spain, Trinidad<br>868-628-1630<br>868-628-5278 (Fax)<br>868-680-3279 (Emergency)<br>http://www.port-of-spain.diplo.de/en/home/index.html |

|  | E-mail: germanembassy@tstt.net.tt  Hours: Monday - Friday 8:00 a.m. - 12:00 p.m. |
|---|---|
| High Commission of India | 6 Victoria Avenue Port of Spain, Trinidad 868-627-7480 868-627-6985 (Fax) http://www.hcipos.org/ |
| Embassy of Brazil | 18 Sweet Briar Road St. Clair, Trinidad 868-622-5779 868-622-4323 (Fax) |
| Embassy of the People's Republic of China | 39 Alexandra St. St. Clair, Trinidad 868-622-6976 868-622-7613 (Fax) |

## Embassies of Trinidad and Tobago to other countries:

| Embassy / Consulate | Contact Information |
|---|---|
| Embassy of the Republic of Trinidad and Tobago - Washington D.C., United States | 1708 Massachusetts Avenue, N.W. Washington D.C. 20036-1975 United States of America 202-467-6490 |

Trinidad

|  |  |
|---|---|
|  | 202-785-3130 (Fax) |
|  | E-mail: embttobago@erols.com |
| Consulate General of the Republic of Trinidad and Tobago<br>- New York, NY USA | 475 Fifth Avenue, 4th Floor<br>New York, N.Y. 10017<br>United States of America<br>212-682-7272<br>212-986-2146 (Fax)<br>E-mail: consulate@ttcgny.com |
| Permanent Mission of the Republic of Trinidad and Tobago to the United Nations<br>- New York, NY USA | 820 Second Avenue, 5th Floor<br>New York, N.Y. 10017<br>United States of America<br>212-697-7620<br>212-682-3580 (Fax)<br>E-mail: tt@un.int |
| Consulate General of the Republic of Trinidad and Tobago<br>- Miami, Florida USA | 1000 Brickell Avenue, Suite 800<br>Miami, Florida 33131-3047<br>United States of America<br>305-374-2199<br>305-374-3199 (Fax)<br>E-mail: ttmiami@worldnet.att.net |
| High Commission of the Republic of Trinidad and Tobago<br>- Ottawa, Canada | 200 First Avenue<br>Ottawa, K1S 2G6,<br>Ontario, Canada<br>613-232-2418<br>613-232-4349 (Fax)<br>http://www.ttmissions.com<br>E-mail: ottawa@ttmissions.com |

| | |
|---|---|
| Consulate General of the Republic of Trinidad and Tobago<br>- Toronto, Canada | 2005 Sheppard Avenue East, Suite 303<br>Willowdale, Ontario M2J 5B4<br>416-495-9442-3<br>416-495-6934 (Fax)<br>E-mail: ttcontor@idirect.com |
| High Commission of the Republic of Trinidad and Tobago<br>- London, England | 42 Belgrave Square<br>London, SW1X 8NT United Kingdom<br>01-144-207-245-9351<br>01-144-207-823-1065 (Fax)<br>E-mail: tthc@btconnect.com |
| Permanent Mission of the Republic of Trinidad and Tobago to the United Nations<br>- Geneva, Switzerland | 37-39 rue de Vermont 1211 Geneva 20, Switzerland<br>011-4122-918-0380<br>011-4122-734-9138 (Fax)<br>http://www.ttperm-mission.ch/<br>E-mail: mission.trinidad-tobago@itu.ch |
| Embassy of the Republic of Trinidad and Tobago<br>- Belgium | Avenue de La Faisanderie 14<br>1150 Brussels, Belgium<br>011 322-762-9400<br>011 322-772-2783 (Fax)<br>E-mail: information@embtrinbago.be |
| Honorary Consul of the Republic of Trinidad and Tobago | Raboisen 3<br>Hamburg 20097 Germany |

Trinidad

| | |
|---|---|
| - Hamburg, Germany | 040-2 20 03 96<br>040-2 20 67 56 (Fax) |
| High Commission of the Republic of Trinidad and Tobago<br>- Nigeria | Plot 1301 Parakou Crescent<br>Off Aminu Kano Crescent Wuse II<br>Abuja F.C.T.<br>Federal Republic of Nigeria<br>011-234-9-523-7534<br>011-234-9-523-7684 (Fax)<br>E-mail: trinitobagoabj@yahoo.co.uk |
| High Commission of the Republic of Trinidad and Tobago<br>- India | 6/25 Shanti Niketan<br>New Delhi, 110021 India<br>011-911-1-2688 8427<br>011-911-1-2688 8463 (Fax)<br>E-mail: hcreptt25@vsn.com |
| Embassy of the Republic of Trinidad and Tobago<br>- Venezuela | Quinta Serrana<br>4ta Avenida Entre 7a Y 8a<br>Transversales Altamira<br>Caracas, Venezuela<br>P.O. Apartado del Este 61322<br>Caracas 1060A, Venezuela<br>011-58-212-261-3748<br>011-58-212-261-9801 (Fax)<br>E-mail: embassytt@cantv.net |
| High Commission of the Republic of Trinidad and Tobago<br>- Jamaica | First Life Building, 3rd Floor<br>60 Knutsford Boulevard<br>Kingston 5 Jamaica |

|  | 876-926-5730 |
|---|---|
|  | 1-876-926-5801 (Fax) |
|  | E-mail: t&thckgn@infochan.com |
| Embassy of the Republic of Trinidad and Tobago - Brazil | QL 02 Conjunto 02 |
|  | Casa 01 71665-028 |
|  | Brasilia D.F. Brazil |
|  | 011-5561-365-3466 |
|  | 011-5561-365-1733 (Fax) |
|  | E-mail: trinbago@terra.com.br |

telephone numbers, emails, and postal addresses are subject to change; check with your local embassy before traveling abroad.

Embassies and consulates can provide helpful assistance to travelers who encounter difficulty while abroad. While you may not have any trouble on vacation on Trinidad and Tobago, it is wise to always carry the contact information for your local embassy or consulate.

# Health
## Staying Healthy on Trinidad
**Vacationers can enjoy their trip and stay healthy**
Traveling to Trinidad and Tobago involves no major health risks. Most health risks that face vacationers when visiting these sister islands can be avoided with a few precautions while enjoying your island retreat.

If you happen to need medical attention while visiting Trinidad and Tobago, be prepared for conditions in health and medical facilities to be more basic than you may be used to. Some areas in the public health care system could use improvements. However, private health care is excellent on the islands, and there are several facilities located on both Trinidad and Tobago. For any emergency situations while on either island, dial 999 or 990 for ambulance service.

This list provides contact information for some hospitals and clinics located on both islands:

| Medical Facility | Telephone Number |
| --- | --- |
| A C I Cath Lab 18 | Elizabeth Street<br>St. Clair<br>868-628-4740 |
| Arima District Hospital | Queen Mary Avenue<br>Arima<br>868-667-0207 |
| Arima Field Clinic | Arima<br>868-667-3479 |
| Aranguez Health Centre | Aranguez<br>868-638-2120 |
| Arouca Health Centre | Arouca<br>868-642-1065 |

| | |
|---|---|
| Auzonville Medical Centre | 11 Eastern Main Road<br>Tunapuna<br>868-654-6437 |
| Bethel Health Centre | Bethel<br>Tobago<br>868-639-8580 |
| Biche Health Centre | Biche<br>868-668-9053 |
| Blanchiesseuse Health Centre | Blanchiesseuse<br>868-669-4118 |
| Brothers Road Health Centre | Princes Town<br>868-642-1065 |
| Caribbean Medical Clinic | 5 Queen's Park East<br>Port of Spain<br>868-625-3944 |
| Diego Martin Health Centre | Diego Martin<br>868-637-9308 |
| Eric Williams Medical Sciences Complex | 1 Mount Hope Medical Complex<br>Mount Hope<br>Port of Spain<br>868-645-4673 |
| Gulf View Medical Centre | Gulf View Link Road<br>San Fernando<br>868-652-7102 |

Trinidad

| | |
|---|---|
| Health Services Chest Clinic | Mt Hope<br>868-645-2640<br><br>San Fernando Chest Clinic<br>San Fernando<br>868-652-3875 |
| Medical Associates Hospital | Albert & Abercromby Streets<br>St. Joseph<br>868-662-2766 |
| Port of Spain Hospital | Port of Spain<br>868-623-2951 |
| Scarborough Health Centre | Scarborough<br>Tobago<br>868-639-2423 |
| Williamsville Health Centre | Princes Town<br>868-655-1751 |

Most doctors require a cash payment after services are rendered. To avoid potentially costly medical bills, check with your health insurance company to see if your policy covers you while traveling abroad. If your insurance doesn't cover your travels, purchase short-term insurance for overseas coverage. Be sure to bring your insurance I.D. card and claims forms for proof of insurance while on Trinidad and Tobago. Travelers don't need any special shots or immunizations to visit Trinidad and Tobago, but it is recommended that vacationers be updated on their immunization boosters, like measles and tetanus, before traveling to any foreign country.

If you require medications, bring an adequate supply with you and keep them in labeled, original containers. If possible, bring a doctor's note describing your condition and medication. If you need a prescription refill or an over-the-counter medicine, several pharmacies are located on the islands. If you are traveling with your prescription medication, make sure they are packaged in their original containors and that they are clearly marked. Additionally, include a prescription slip or note from your physician.

| Pharmacy | Phone Number |
| --- | --- |
| Dove Drugs | 868-639-2976 |
| PharmaRx Pharmacy | 868-631-1030 |
| Ross Budget Drugs Ltd. | 868-639-2658 |
| Scarborough Drugs | 868-639-4161 |
| Tobago Pharmacy | 868-639-3784 |
| Tri-Pharmacy | 868-639-6825 |
| Tsoi's Pharmacy | 868-639-3383 |

The most common illnesses that affect vacationers are mostly preventable. Heed these precautions to stay healthy on your island getaway:

- Trinidad and Tobago are very close to the equator, and the sun can get extremely hot. Wear sunscreen with the appropriate SPF to protect your skin from harmful UV rays, and drink plenty of water and fluids to prevent dehydration when spending time in the sun;
- While in the waters surrounding the island, be cautious of sea urchins and jelly fish that can cause nasty skin injuries;
- Mosquitoes and other pesky insects can be irritating as well as cause minor skin irritation. Don't forget to wear bug repellent when spending time outdoors.

Seasoned travelers will suggest that you pack a Travel Medical Kit, filled with supplies to treat minor ailments. This should include the following:

- Painkillers including acetaminophen, aspirin, ibuprofen;
- Antihistamines;
- Topical disinfectant;

- ➢ Antacids;
  Rubbing alcohol;
- ➢ Bandages;
- ➢ Thermometer.

Vacationers can enjoy their retreat to Trinidad and Tobago while staying healthy by simply remembering to follow a few health and medical precautions.

# Hours of Operation

## Have the Time of Your Life on Trinidad
**Keeping up with the hours of operation will help travelers take care of business**
Whether you have important business to conduct or even attractions you don't want to miss, it's useful to know how long businesses stay open on Trinidad or Tobago.

### Banks

There are four major banks that operate on both islands. These banks all keep the same schedule: 8:00 a.m. to 2:00 p.m Monday through Thursday and 9:00 a.m. to 12:00 p.m. and 3:00 p.m. until 5:00 p.m. on Fridays. Banks on the island are generally not open for business on Saturdays and Sundays, but banking facilities in shopping malls and busier areas may stay open until 6:00 p.m. or 7:00 p.m.

## Shopping

Shopping is a major attraction to the both Trinidad and Tobago, and many vacationers enjoy taking advantage of great buys from all over the world. Travelers will find that the shops and bazaars on the islands have hours that can accommodate most vacationers' shopping needs. Most shops are open Monday through Saturday. On weekends, shops are open from 8:00 a.m. to 4:30 p.m. and 8:00 a.m. until noon on Saturdays. Malls and some larger shops are open longer on the weekdays and all day on Saturdays.

## Post Offices

Vacationers who want to send a post card or package will find the post offices on Trinidad and Tobago keep odd hours. Post offices are only open on the weekdays, so prepare your mail and parcels before the weekend. Offices are open from 8:00 a.m. to 12:00 p.m., and they reopen at 1:00 p.m. until 4:00 p.m.

Tourist will find that they can take care of most of their business and pleasure priorities on Trinidad and Tobago at mostly convenient times.

# Languages

## Can We Talk on Trinidad?
**Travelers will encounter a variety of English dialects on Trinidad and Tobago**

English is the official language of Trinidad and Tobago, but English-speaking visitors may still have difficulty understanding local speech. With several different dialects and many cultures merging on these islands, you are likely to hear English spoken with a twist or two.

There are a wide variety of cultures and nationalities of people found on Trinidad and Tobago. These two vacation paradises are the most cosmopolitan islands in the Caribbean, with a population that includes Syrians, Chinese, Americans, Europeans, East Indians, and Parsees just to name a few of the cultures on the island. Because natives are descended from nations all over the world, English is spoken with many different accents and the local dialect of Trinibagianese.

Locals speak quickly, which can result in difficulty understanding. There are some expressions used by locals that are helpful to know when traveling to Trinidad or Tobago. If a local invites you for a "lime," you're not about to eat a sour fruit, you're being invited to a party, and while at a "lime," you may be asked to "wine," which is a dance done by rotating the hips. If you want to chill out on your island vacation, the phrase to know is "limin" which means relaxing and having a good time.

While vacationing on Trinidad and Tobago, you are sure to hear English phrases mixed with the islands' diverse dialect and idiomatic phrases.

# Passports

## What Do I Need to enter Trinidad?
**Visitors need important documentation to enter the country**
Business travelers, students, and tourists must all carry very specific documentation in order to enter any foreign country, including Trinidad and Tobago. Many visitors will only require a passport and return plane ticket.

**Entry Requirements**

Business travelers and tourists traveling to Trinidad and Tobago from the United States and the European Union will find that visiting the islands for periods up to three months is relatively easy. Visitors from these areas will not need a visa but are required to produce a valid passport that does not expire within three months of the planned date of departure from Trinidad and Tobago, as well as a return or onward ticket to a destination outside of the country. Travelers who will be staying in the country for more than three months or for reasons other than business or tourism should consult their embassy for information on visas and permits. Due to the 2005 enactied Western

Hemisphere Travel Initiative, travelers from the United States and North America who wish to re-enter or visit the United States must have a valid passport to do so.

Travelers from countries outside of the United States and the European Union must have passports that are valid for six months past their travel date and a return plane ticket. Two visa applications, available at http://www.gov.tt/services/, along with two recent passport photos, must be submitted. Business travelers must also produce an official company letter explaining their travel.

**Getting Hitched**
Couples who are planning on getting married on Trinidad and Tobago will also need to produce several important documents to receive clearance to marry. Travelers must have passports and airline tickets, and both must be on Trinidad and Tobago for a full three days before the planned wedding ceremony. Marriage participants should also be able to produce documents proving name change, divorce, or death of a former spouse. Licenses and certificates cost about $55(USD). For current information on getting married on Trinidad and Tobago, contact:

| Contact | Contact Information |
| --- | --- |
| Registrar General's Office, Trinidad | Registrar House |

|  |  |
|---|---|
|  | 72 - 74 South Quay |
|  | Port of Spain, Trinidad |
|  | 868-623-7163 |
| Warden's Office, Tobago | Inland Revenue Bldg |
|  | Sangster's Hill |
|  | Scarborough, Tobago |
|  | 868-639-2410 |
| Registrar General's Office, Tobago | Jerningham St |
|  | Scarborough, Tobago |
|  | 868-639-3210 |

Any travelers arriving at Trinidad and Tobago from a yellow-fever area within a five-day time period must have a vaccination certificate.

Whether you are traveling for business, romance, or tourism, preparing your documents to enter Trinidad and Tobago should be easy and well worth the effort.

## Postal Services

### Trinidad Post Card Madness
**Travelers will find their share of post offices on Trinidad and Tobago**
With many post office locations throughout the islands, sending postcards, letters, and packages from Trinidad and Tobago is easy.

Main post office branches are open in Trinidad's capital, Port of Spain, and Tobago's capital, Scarborough. Along with the main post offices, these postal branches are located on both islands:

| Post Office | Phone Number |
|---|---|
| Couva Post Office - Trinidad | 868- 636-2560 |
| Charlotteville Post Office - Tobago | 868-660-4355 |
| Moriah Post Office - Tobago | 868-660-0884 |
| Roxborough Post Office - Tobago | 868-660-4322 |
| Scarborough Post Office - Tobago | 868-660-7377 |
| Speyside Post Office - Tobago | 868-660-5569 |
| New National Mail Centre - Trinidad | 868-669-5361 |
| Arima Post Office - Trinidad | 868-667-3221 |
| Belmont Post Office - Trinidad | 868-624-7794 |

Trinidad

| | |
|---|---|
| Blundell Post Office - Trinidad | 868-625-1828 |
| Carenage Post Office - Trinidad | 868-632-1834 |
| Caroni Post Office - Trinidad | 868-662-7123 |
| Cedros Post Office - Trinidad | 868-648-2923 |
| Central Market Post Office - Trinidad | 868-623-5210 |
| Chaguanas Post Office - Trinidad | 868-665-5292 |
| Chaguaramas Post Office - Trinidad | 868-634-1034 |
| City Gate Post Office - Trinidad | 868-684-687 |
| Claxton Bay Post Office - Trinidad | 868-659-2209 |
| Couva Post Office - Trinidad | 868-636-2560 |
| Cumuto Post Office - Trinidad | 868-643-9856 |
| Cunupia Post Office | 868-665-3567 |

| | |
|---|---|
| - Trinidad | |
| Curepe Post Office - Trinidad | 868-662-4653 |
| Diego Martin Post Office - Trinidad | 868-637-9870 |
| El Socorro Post Office - Trinidad | 868-638-6754 |
| Erin Post Office - Trinidad | 868-649-8732 |
| Excellent Stores Post Office - Trinidad | 868-623-5321 |
| Freeport Post Office - Trinidad | 868-678-9172 |
| Fyzabad Post Office 0 - Trinidad | 868-677-747 |
| Gasparillo Post Office - Trinidad | 868-650-2205 |
| Gonzales Post Office 1 - Trinidad | 868-625-472 |
| General Post Office (GPO) - Trinidad | 868-625-5550 |
| Gran Couva Post Office - Trinidad | 868-679-9469 |

Trinidad

| Post Office | Phone |
|---|---|
| Gulf City Post Office - Trinidad | 868-657-6185 |
| La Brea Post Office - Trinidad | 868-648-7581 |
| La Horquetta Post Office - Trinidad | 868-643-5033 |
| La Romain Post Office - Trinidad | 868-652-0900 |
| Laventille Post Office - Trinidad | 868-623-8165 |
| Marabella Post Office - Trinidad | 868-658-5602 |
| New Grant Post Office - Trinidad | 868-655-8734 |
| Oropouche Post Office - Trinidad | 868-677-7414 |
| Piarco Post Office - Trinidad | 868-669-4333 |
| St Anns Post Office - Trinidad | 868-625-2669 |
| Williamsville Post Office - Trinidad | 868-655-2149 |

For post office customer service, dial 800-POST(800-7678). For courier service, 800-SEND(800-7363). Post offices are open 8:00 a.m. to 12:00 p.m., are closed one hour until 1:00 p.m., then stay open until 4:30 p.m. Monday through Friday.

Costs of sending mail from either island depend on the mail's destination and how large it is. Generally, postage to the United States and Canada costs about $3.45(TT) for first-class letters and $2.25(TT) for postcards. Prices may be slightly higher for other destinations. When sending postage to or from Trinidad and Tobago, you will not need a ZIP code on either island. Just label the mail with the address of the establishment, the town, and 'Trinidad and Tobago, West Indies'.

Mail circulation on Trinidad and Tobago may be considered slow compared to some larger countries, and you may arrive home before your package. Airmail from the Caribbeans takes approximately seven to 14 days to reach the United States and Canada, and surface mail can take up to six weeks. Airmail going to the United Kingdom, Australia, or New Zealand can take from 2 to 4 weeks.

With so many post offices located on Trinidad and Tobago, you should have no trouble sending mail and packages back home.

# Telephones

## Want to Talk on Trinidad?
**Making a phone call while on vacation is generally hassle-free**
You don't have to feel disconnected during your vacation. Trinidad and Tobago have a sleepy natural beauty, but the tropical islands are also technologically up-to-date with advanced communications systems.

Telephones are available all over Trinidad and Tobago and at most hotels and guesthouses. The area code on the islands is 868, which also happens to spell out "TNT" on the key pad. To call Trinidad from the United States and Canada, dial 1 and the area code. The country code is the same as the are code for travelers calling from other countries. Placing a local call on both islands is as easy as dialing the seven-digit number.

Vacationers should be able to place international calls from most hotels and resorts, most of which will allow you to place a direct international call. Many hotels charge hefty fees for overseas calls, so you may want to invest in a calling card, especially if you plan to make several international phone calls.

To place a call from Trinidad or Tobago to the United States or Canada, dial 1, the area code, and the number. Travelers calling Europe or any other country should check the appropriate direct-dial codes in the phone directory in order to place a call. The country code for the

United States and Canada is 1; Australia, 61; New Zealand, 64; and the United Kingdom, 44.

To use a pay phone on either of the islands, you will have to purchase a companion card, which allows you to make calls from any pay phone on Trinidad and Tobago, including from your hotel. Companion cards are available at most shops and can be purchased in a variety of denominations. Cellular phones also work on the islands, as well as Internet service.

# Time Zones

### Time Zones of Trinidad
**Trinidad and Tobago does not observe daylight savings time**
Most travelers to Trinidad and Tobago quickly acclimate themselves to the climate and time change on the islands. Once you settle into the relaxing life on "Caribbean time," you too will be quick to forget your jet lag.

The time on Trinidad and Tobago is four hours behind Greenwich Mean Time, placing it in the Atlantic Standard Time zone. This means that visitors from the United Kingdom and most of Europe will experience time changes of four to six hours. Time on the islands is one hour ahead of Eastern Standard Time observed on the East Coast of the United States. Trinidad and Tobago, do not, however, observe daylight-saving time, which means that in April through October, the time on Trinidad and Tobago will be the same as destinations observing Eastern Standard Time.

Here is a sampling of time differences for travelers from throughout the globe:

## At 12:00 p.m. on Trinidad and Tobago

| City Called | Local Time |
|---|---|
| Brussels | 5:00 p.m. (plus 1 hour in daylight savings) |
| Copenhagen | 5:00 p.m. (plus 1 hour in daylight savings) |
| Hong Kong | 12:00 a.m. (next day) |
| Istanbul | 6:00 p.m. (plus 1 hour in daylight savings) |
| Los Angeles | 8:00 a.m. (plus 1 hour in daylight savings) |
| London | 4:00 p.m. |
| Madrid | 5:00 p.m. (plus 1 hour in daylight savings) |
| Moscow | 7:00 p.m. (plus 1 hour in daylight savings) |

| Paris | 5:00 p.m. (plus 1 hour in daylight savings) |
|---|---|
| Sydney | 3:00 a.m. (minus 1 hour in daylight savings) |
| Tokyo | 1:00 a.m. (next day) |

Travelers from around the world come to Trinidad and Tobago to enjoy beaches and Carnival, and most find the time difference to be only a minor issue.

# Tipping

## How Then Shall We Tip on Trinidad?
**Tipping is a good way to show appreciation for a service well done**
On Trinidad and Tobago, tipping is considered a gesture of kindness and gratitude for a service well done. Most on the islands do not expect vacationers to tip, but if you choose to, your gesture will be welcomed warmly.

You will require the services of waiters, cab drivers, and hotel personnel while enjoying your vacation. The prices on Trinidad and Tobago are generally lower than the rest of the islands in the Caribbean, where tipping and gratuity is often a part of their tradition. Accommodations and restaurant prices are extremely affordable, and many dining establishments have prices that cater to local incomes, which are low, rather than higher.

While staying in any of Trinidad and Tobago's hotels or resorts, you will be required to pay a government tax of 15 percent along with a 10 percent service charge, which will be added to your final bill. Housekeepers and bellhops may not expect a tip for their service, but just because it isn't obligatory doesn't mean it isn't appreciated.

Most restaurants also add a 10 percent service charge to bills, which is standard on both islands. If this charge is not applied to your final bill, you are not required to tip, but a gratuity is encouraged, and a tip of 15 percent is the usual amount given. If your waiter has done a particularly good job, you may want to be more generous.

Vacationers should negotiate the fare of their taxi cab ride before setting off. Fares may or may not include gratuity. Most drivers don't expect a tip, but you should consider the length of your cab journey as well as whether your driver acted as a tour guide. There is no expected amount or percentage that should be given, but if you received good service, leave the driver a few extra dollars.

Vacationers can show their appreciation for services they receive on the island by leaving a generous tip, which is not expected but is always greatly appreciated.

# Tourist Offices

## Tourist Offices on Trinidad

**Vacationers may find that tourist offices have helpful information about their vacation destination**

Finding information on your upcoming vacation is an important part to planning your trip. There are several sources of information that vacationers can take advantage of to learn more about your island retreat to Trinidad and Tobago.

Travelers who questions or just want to find out more about Trinidad and Tobago have to offer will find that contacting a tourist office will be helpful in discovering useful facts and information about these to beautiful islands. Here is a list of tourist offices located in several different countries and on Trinidad and Tobago:

| Tourist Office | Location and Contact Info |
| --- | --- |
| Trinidad & Tobago Tourism Office | Contact Jane West or Nova Alexander<br>800-804-8787<br>E-mail: trinbago@ihml.com<br>http://www.visittnt.com |
| Trinidad & Tobago Hotel & Tourism Association - Tobago | PO Box 295<br>Scarborough, Tobago<br>868-639-9543<br>868-660-8228 (Fax) |

Trinidad

|  |  |
|---|---|
|  | E-mail: tthtatob@tstt.net.tt |
| Trinidad & Tobago Tourist Office<br>- USA - New York | Keating Communications Inc.<br>350 Fifth Avenue<br>New York, NY 10118<br>212-760-2400<br>212-760-6402 (Fax) |
| Trinidad & Tobago Tourist Office<br>- USA - Florida | Cheryl Andrews Marketing Inc.<br>1500 San Remo, Suite 145<br>Coral Gables Florida 33146<br>305-663-1660<br>305-666-9728 (Fax) |
| Trinidad & Tobago Tourist Office<br>- Canada | The RMR Group Inc.<br>Taurus House<br>512 Duplex Ave,<br>Toronto, M4R 2E3<br>416-485-8724<br>416-485-8256 (Fax) |
| British High Commission on Trinidad | PO Box 778<br>19 St Clair Avenue<br>St Clair Port of Spain<br>Trinidad<br>868-622-2748<br>868-622-4555 (Fax)<br>E-mail: ppabhc@opus.co.tt |
| High Commission for the Republic of Trinidad & Tobago | 42 Belgrave Square<br>London SW1X 8NT<br>(020) 7245 9351 |

| - United Kingdom | (020) 7823 1065 (Fax) |
| --- | --- |
|  | E-mail: tthc.info@virgin.net |

Trinidad and Tobago are full of gorgeous beaches and vibrant festivals and events. Tourist offices can help travelers map their tropical adventure to these lively islands.

# Weather on Trinidad

Travelers can expect warm temperatures year-round on Trinidad and Tobago

Many vacationers looking for a hot time in a tropical paradise will enjoy soaking up the sun in beautiful Trinidad and Tobago.

These two lovely vacation spots are the southernmost islands in the West Indies, and they are closer to the equator than the other islands in the Caribbean, which means that temperatures can rise. These sister islands maintain a tropical climate all year long, which makes them the perfect place to vacation almost any time.

The tropical temperatures range from moderate to hot on Trinidad and Tobago, and they only slightly vary throughout the year. The islands' climate is moderated by the constant northeastern tradewinds, which keep the temperature at a steamy 84 degrees

Fahrenheit during daytime hours. Nighttime temperatures drop to a cool and comfortable 72 degrees Fahrenheit. Tobago's temperatures are slightly cooler than Trinidad's because it receives more of the tradewinds breezes. Travelers shouldn't worry about the temperatures fluctuating too much because it rarely reaches above 90 degrees Fahrenheit, and temperatures rarely dip below 70.

Trinidad and Tobago have two seasons: summer and winter. The seasons are not as distinguishable by differences in temperature than they are by rainfall, though winter is slightly cooler. The islands experience more rain during winter, or the wet season, which makes the temperatures on the islands cooler than during the drier summer. Wet season falls from June to December, which is also the low tourist season. Most of the country experiences about 40 inches of annual rainfall, which is mostly attributed to short bursts of showers.

A little bit of rain shouldn't stop vacationers from visiting Trinidad and Tobago during this time of year because showers usually don't last more than a couple of hours, and then the beautiful Caribbean sun comes back out, shining brightly. Hurricane season is during the rainy months, but Trinidad and Tobago are both located below the hurricane belt, and the islands generally experience less storm activity than some of the other islands in the Caribbean. The biggest problem with traveling to the islands during the winter season are the bugs, which tend to be worse during the rainy season. Visitors should remember to wear plenty of bug repellent while enjoying the islands gorgeous outdoors.

The dry season is from January to May, when weather is colder in northern regions, and travelers come to take advantage of ample sunshine and warm Caribbean weather.

| Month | Avg. Daily High Temp (Degrees Fahrenheit) | Avg. Daily Low Temp (Degrees Fahrenheit) | Avg. Monthly Precipitation (inches) | % Days with Rain |
|---|---|---|---|---|
| January | 85.0 | 71.0 | 2.8 | 61.0 |
| February | 86.0 | 71.0 | 1.7 | 58.5 |
| March | 87.0 | 72.0 | 1.2 | 48.1 |
| April | 88.0 | 74.0 | 1.8 | 47.8 |
| May | 88.0 | 75.0 | 4.4 | 65.3 |
| June | 86.0 | 75.0 | 10.0 | 80.8 |
| July | 87.0 | 74.0 | 9.8 | 75.8 |
| August | 88.0 | 74.0 | 9.4 | 72.0 |
| September | 88.0 | 74.0 | 7.2 | 63.8 |
| October | 87.0 | 74.0 | 7.0 | 62.9 |

| | | | | |
|---|---|---|---|---|
| November | 87.0 | 74.0 | 7.8 | 70.5 |
| December | 85.0 | 72.0 | 5.8 | 68.5 |
| Annual | 87.0 | 73.0 | 69.7 | 64.6 |

The sultry and tantalizing weather of Trinidad and Tobago make these charming Caribbean islands an unforgettable vacationing spot any time of year.

# Weddings on Trinidad

## Choosing a wedding on Trinidad and Tobago is the first step to planning the perfect day

Couples seeking an unforgettable wedding experience, should consider planning to host their big event in beautiful Trinidad and Tobago. From exquisite landscapes and perfect climate conditions to delicious food and a superb locale for a built-in honeymoon, a wedding event on Trinidad and Tobago promises to deliver memories to last a lifetime.

If you have always imagined getting married on a sandy stretch of beach in the Caribbean, but never believed it could be plausible, think again. A small amount of research and large dose of mindful organization can enable you to have the Caribbean wedding you've always dreamed about.

**Pros and Cons**

Some men and women find that wedding event planning can be quite stressful, notably when you choose to place all your confidence in an event manager in a foreign nation. However, for so many couples, the advantages outnumber the disadvantages. Still, a Caribbean wedding isn't for everyone. The included list of pros and cons may help you to determine if getting married on Trinidad and Tobago is appropriate for you.

**Pros**

➢ Cost. While many individuals do not recognize this, a destination wedding could actually save you money - including the expenses of airfare. This is because destination weddings are likely to be smaller affairs at which less people attend, thus costing you less money in table settings and cuisine. Numerous resorts also provide wedding and honeymoon package promotions, thus enhancing your savings even more.

➢ Weather. While thinking about a destination wedding, many couples are enticed by Trinidad and Tobago because of its tropical weather conditions, where the average temperature

## Trinidad

rarely dips below 72 degrees Fahrenheit throughout the year. Rain storms do occur, but they are usually over before they begin.

- ➢ Planning. Couples preparing for a destination wedding usually choose an event planner (or one is allocated to you by your resort when you buy a wedding package from them). This helps ensure that every single element of your big day is thoughtfully considered by an expert.

- ➢ Friends and Family. Arranging a destination wedding means that you can trim down your guest list - you don't have to feel compelled to invite a relative you aren't very close to, or your fiancé's boss.

**Cons**

- ➢ Cost. While researching a destination wedding, many couples may feel that they are responsible for handling all travel expenses for their entire wedding party. If you decide to include all these expenses within your budget, a Caribbean wedding will undoubtedly require a larger budget.

- ➢ Weather. It is important to keep in mind that because of Trinidad and Tobago's location within the hurricane belt, scheduling a wedding celebration during hurricane season (from the beginning of June until the end of November) presents a slight risk.

- Planning. Since you will not have the option to personally check out and choose wedding particulars for much of the time leading up to your nuptials, you may find yourself becoming nervous because you feel that you are not able to exercise as much control over everything.
- Legal issues. Legislation pertaining to marriage licenses could be different than those you would deal with back home. Procuring a marriage license on Trinidad and Tobago necessitates time, so a rapidly organized wedding might not be practical.
- Family and friends. It is important that couples keep in mind that everyone you want to share your wedding memories with may not be able to attend a Caribbean wedding due to obligations that may prevent them from being able to travel.

**Why Choose Trinidad and Tobago**

Out of all the locations in the world, why should you choose to get married on Trinidad and Tobago? The answer is simple really: the ambiance. Trinidad and Tobago mixes a cosmopolitan atmosphere with a laid back, tropical environment. On one island, Trinidad, guests will experience the upbeat, artistic lifestyles of the islanders that is surrounded by lush greenery and the crystal, cool waters of the Caribbean. Meanwhile, Tobago offers an old world feel, the island dense with history, mythology, and the pride of those who live there. The diversity of the islands allows for varied wedding locales and set-ups; from indoor affairs to beach side vows.

Furthermore, the activities you can plan on the days surrounding your wedding are endless. Days spent participating in water sports on the Beaches beach will allow for an opportunity to release all of the tension that typically surrounds wedding planning, while touring historic landmarks and natural sites will make great memories.

**Local Wedding Customs**

An elegant way to incorporate the customs of Trinidad and Tobago into your wedding is through your attire. At a traditional ceremony on the islands, the groom will wear a black suit complete with top hat, bow tie, and tails over a white shirt, while the bride will wear a dress made of satin (usually white, but pale pinks and other light colors are common as well).

If you have your own ideas of how you would like to dress, another great way to highlight local culture is by serving up some regional fare, such as dumplings and crab, stuffed crab, and rotis (bread stuffed with chickpea curry and ground meats).

## Types of Ceremonies

As you start the process of wedding planning, you can compose a memorable event that is ideal for your desires by choosing a venue in which you will feel most comfortable in. If religious beliefs and tradition are fundamental to you, planning a traditional wedding event at an island church, or perhaps a historic landmark may work best for you. If you're a dreamer at heart, imagine an outdoor wedding on the beach, in a garden, or at the edge of a waterfall. Couples seeking adventure, however, may prefer a wedding underwater or at the top of a mountain. No matter where you imagine your perfect wedding, Trinidad and Tobago has a venue to suit your tastes.

## Budgeting

Despite the fact that a Caribbean wedding generally is less expensive than an elaborate event hosted back home, it is still imperative that you take some time to sit down and create a budget. Plan with your fiancée and create a list of everything you believe you will end up spending funds on, in order of relevance to you. Some typical ideas include the catering, location, photographer, and dress, among many others. After doing some quick research, allocate an estimated price to each item, then total everything up. This will provide you with a rough idea of what you can plan on spending. Remember that this total will alter as you shop for your big event, and the organized list of vital items will help you to know immediately what items you can trim back on and which items you simply can't be without.

**Requirements**

Couples wishing to obtain a marriage license on Trinidad and Tobago must visit the Trinidad Registrar General's Office or the Tobago Warden's Office at least three days after their arrival on the island, and 24 hours before their wedding. With them they should bring $51(USD) to pay for their license, plus the following documents: certified copies of birth certificates, death certificates, divorce certificates, adoption papers, and passport.

Planning a wedding on Trinidad and Tobago doesn't have to be a daunting prospect. Although you will be celebrating your big day far from home, the beauty and enchantment of the islands are sure to make all the time you spent planning worth it. Take each aspect of planning step-by-step, weigh your options, and your wedding on Trinidad and Tobago is sure to be a dream come true.

# Budgeting & Planning

## Budgeting for a Wedding on Trinidad
**First decide on Trinidad and Tobago for your wedding, then set your budget, and go from there**

Whether you choose to say your vows on the lively Trinidad or the laid-back Tobago, the perfect ambiance for your destination wedding is only a plane ride away. After you have made the decision to go for an island wedding, you're ready to start organizing your big event.

What is the biggest secret to achieving a great Trinidad and Tobago wedding? The key is to begin the planning process as quickly as possible. A good system of time management should be developed because it allows you to save time when researching choices, making reservations, and coping with any complications that may arise. Beginning early also gives you time to take advantage of any possible deals that could become available.

**Hired Help**

Most couples who are planning a wedding on Trinidad and Tobago find that the most significant obstacle is making the arrangements from afar. Many hire a wedding or event planner to do what they do best - make the planning of their wedding as stress free and simple as possible. You can hire someone local to you, someone on Trinidad and Tobago, or choose to buy a resort wedding package.

If you choose to hire a wedding planner, make sure he or she has previous experience planning a Caribbean wedding and has references available. Connections in the area and knowledge of the local language and customs will help guarantee that your experience is exactly what you want and expect. Remember, if you want your wedding planner to be on site the day of your wedding, be prepared to to pay for his or her airfare and hotel stay.

A large number of couples find that choosing an event planner on Trinidad and Tobago is a great way to ensure that they have someone on the island to be their eyes and ears. This person will be able to handle every detail of your wedding, and most importantly analyze venues and vendors in person.

Wedding packages offered by local are most common and often the most reliable. Accommodations, venue, officiant, catering, adornments, and more are usually included in one flat rate. Read our guide to Trinidad and Tobago Wedding Locations and Venues noted at the bottom of this page for more information on resort weddings.

**How to Plan a Trinidad and Tobago Wedding Yourself**
Preparing a Trinidad and Tobago wedding may seem stressful but many find it a fun challenge and have successfully achieved their

dream event. Stay prepared, write lists, and keep notes of every phone call and transaction you make.

## Step One: Structure Your Budget

Developing a sensible budget is essential to any successful island wedding. On average, couples in the United States spend between $20,000 and $30,000 on their big day, while a wedding on Trinidad and Tobago can cost you as little as $2,000. Numerous major resorts and **hotels** have wedding planning services that can prepare your big event down to the very last detail, and charge a single set fee for the entire package. If you decide to arrange the entire wedding yourself, consider the expenses you may encounter.

| ESTIMATED TRINIDAD AND TOBAGO WEDDING COSTS | |
|---|---|
| Item | Expected Cost |
| Marriage License | $55(USD) |
| Officiant | $50 to $250(USD) |
| Photography | $500 to $3000(USD) |
| Flowers | $300 to $1500(USD) |
| Decorations | $300 to $1500(USD) |
| Venue | $0 to $1000(USD) |
| Food | $25 to $50(USD) per person |

| | |
|---|---|
| Lodging | $100+(USD) per night |

The chart above merely addresses wedding basics, and estimates are based upon average costs of the individual items. Consider other fundamentals such as the bride's gown, the groom's tuxedo, and the wedding rings. Overall, wedding costs will change drastically depending on which items you decide are the most important. You need to stay within a reasonable budget that is based upon your financial situation. List items commonly associated with a wedding from maximum value to lowest value and allocate a price estimate to each item.

Items ranked in order of importance will allow you to see exactly where you may be willing to trim back and where you aren't willing to compromise.

**Step Two: Select a Theme**

By this point you will have determined what style of wedding you would love to host, and the type of venue you would like to have it in. These selections will quickly trim down your list of potential vendors. Keep in mind that there are numerous islands that make up Trinidad and Tobago, and that you should determine upon which island you would like to get married early on. Consult our guide to Trinidad and

Tobago Wedding Locations and Venues for more information about the types of weddings available.

**Step Three: Do Your Research**

Every location, vendor, resort, decoration, and method of transportation should be evaluated. Contact companies for price estimates and inform them that you are arranging your nuptials from abroad, and that they should expect many long distance phone calls and e-mail communications. When you contract vendors sight unseen, ask for references from those who have previously used their services.

Also give consideration to the time of year in which you wish to get married, and the type of festivals and events that may occur during that time. If you want you and your guests to experience a party environment, getting married on Trinidad and Tobago during Carnival, for example, may be just the ticket. However, if you would rather have an intimate, discreet event, you should make other arrangements.

While you are researching vendors and venues, take a break and take some time to enlighten yourself on the typical wedding traditions of the islands. You may be inspired to incorporate some of these customs into your own ceremony. Try serving local foods at your reception, or carrying a bouquet of Trinidad and Tobago's national flower, the pride of Trinidad, down the aisle.

**Step Four: Book Your Vendors**

The vendors you select will essentially make or break your wedding event. When you make your final decisions and book your vendors, explain precisely what you are looking for, and the dates you have chosen. Get all of your price quotes in writing (have them send you a quote through the post office, by e-mail, or by fax). Keep duplicates of everything including invoices of all items that are included in the price. Some businesses require a deposit. Do not send anyone payments until you have received a paper statement. Protect yourself from any possible misunderstandings.

**Step Five: Take Care of at Home Projects**

Many couples wish to bring a bit of personal flair to their Trinidad and Tobago wedding. If you are creating or purchasing any of your wedding decorations at home, there is no better time than now to start working on this project. This may also be the time to purchase the wedding dress and/or make arrangements to rent a tuxedo. List everything you plan on taking care of at home, and the estimated time it will take you to accomplish it.

Now is also the time to gather together the documents that you need to bring with you to Trinidad and Tobago in order to obtain your marriage license. Getting married on the islands is rather easy; couples simply stay on the island for three days before bringing proof of birth and marital status to the Registrar General's office. Learn more about the process by reading our guide to Trinidad Wedding Requirements and Traditions.

**Step Six: Follow Up**

Although you may think your arrangements are finalized, it is still important to talk to your vendors periodically to review their progress, or to discuss any changes that need to be made. Don't worry about calling too often. They are working for you, and you are paying them to provide these services.

Listed below are a few additional tips that will assist you in planning your Trinidad and Tobago wedding.

➢ Consider the weather. If you are planning a wedding at an outdoor venue, make alternative arrangements in case of stormy conditions. Typical weather conditions for that time of year should be considered when choosing your wedding attire. If you plan to marry on the beach in the middle of a hot afternoon, plan accordingly.

> Send wedding supplies ahead of time. If you are bringing any wedding items with you from home, consider shipping them ahead to your resort or venue so that you can avoid airport hassles and restrictions. Be sure to arrange for insurance on these items in case they are lost or damaged during shipment.

Rather than feeling tense and anxious during the days leading up to your wedding celebration, make organization your ally. Whether you choose to plan your Trinidad and Tobago wedding on your own, or enlist the help of professionals, following the guidelines listed here will ensure that you keep your planning done in an organized, practical, and stress-free fashion.

## Locations & Venues

### Wedding Locations and Venues on Trinidad
**Planning a wedding on Trinidad and Tobago will prove there is no wrong place to get married on the islands**
In choosing Trinidad and Tobago as their wedding destination, couples get to choose between two very different islands for their ceremony: the city-like Trinidad and the more Eco-friendly Tobago. After deciding upon which island to say their vows, couples then have multitudes of venue options, from outdoor gardens to a more traditional church setting.

Locating a wedding venue without being able to physically visit the location prior to booking it is one of the toughest challenges faced by couples planning a wedding on Trinidad and Tobago. Due to this major obstacle, many people prefer to solicit the assistance of an event planner to take care of every necessary element surrounding a wedding. If you prefer to do all the organizing on your own, figuring out the kind of wedding you would like to have will assist you to trim down your choices considerably, making the whole task a little less overwhelming.

## Choosing an Island
### Trinidad
Trinidad is more populated than Tobago, and has a livelier vibe. The island is filled with open-air markets, night clubs, and street performers perfecting their steel-pan skills. That is not to say that Trinidad is lacking in physical beauty. Beaches, gardens, and historic sites offer picturesque wedding sites. Trinidad is the best locale for couples who want their island wedding to be a celebration of their love, and who imagine the days surrounding their big day to be filled with site-seeing, clubbing, and energetic local events.

### Tobago
It can be easily be said that Tobago is the opposite of Trinidad. This is the island couples go to for quiet, relaxation, and a more down-to-

earth atmosphere. As one of the top Eco-tourism islands in the Caribbean, couples won't have to doubt that an outdoor wedding on Tobago would be a thing of beauty - and the days leading up to their vows would allow the couple to participate in adventurous activities such as hiking and diving, or transversely, completely relaxing moments lying on the beach.

**Types of Ceremonies**

A wedding ceremony on Trinidad and Tobago can be anything you want it to be. Although the most commonly encountered type of wedding planned by travelers is a beach front ceremony, this is by no means the only option available.

**Traditional Wedding**

Many couples desire a traditional style of wedding, which usually takes place in a religious establishment, with relatives and friends filling the pews as the bride slowly walks down the aisle toward her waiting groom. Once the vows are said, the wedding party and their guests usually gather at a dining or banquet hall to celebrate the big event. This is as much a possibility on Trinidad and Tobago as anywhere else. Your wedding planner can help you to find a chapel or temple that that accommodates your religious preferences.

In addition to religious buildings, couples may choose to celebrate with a more traditionally designed ceremony at a gallery, plantation house, or significant historical site such as the Stollmeyer Castle on Trinidad.

## Outdoor Wedding

As previously mentioned, the seashore is the most common location to have a destination wedding. It goes without saying that a wedding ceremony performed on the beach is an exquisite affair. With so many natural beauties like fine sand and exotic foliage surrounding you, you'll find that very few additional decorations are necessary. Beach weddings are also very simple to plan, and small weddings may not even need permits.

If you dream of getting married in an outdoor environment, beaches are not the only venue available for your big day. Countless hotels and offer villas with views of seashores, hills, and tropical vegetation. Getting married in a botanical garden is another alternative. For something especially extraordinary and spectacular, consider planning a wedding with a waterfall as your backdrop.

| OUTDOOR WEDDING VENUES ON TRINIDAD AND TOBAGO | | |
|---|---|---|
| Venue | Location | Phone Number |

Trinidad

| Botanical Gardens | Trinidad | 868-622-6423 |
| Caroni Bird Sandtuary | Trinidad | 868-645-1305 |
| Fort George | Trinidad | 868-675-7034 |
| Main Ridge Forest Reserve | Tobago | N/A |
| San Fernando Hill | Trinidad | N/A |

## Marriage at Sea

Have you always fantasized about getting married at sea? Trinidad and Tobago present the ideal place for an oceanic exchange of vows. The Caribbean Sea offers some of the most crystal clear, calm waters, and amazing views. You could possibly decide to get married on board a major cruise line that makes a visit to Trinidad and Tobago, or chartera yacht for a few hours. You may even book the boat for the entire day and host your reception on the vessel as well.

## Casual vs. Formal

Every couple has a different view in relation to how formal they would like their wedding ceremony to be. Though island weddings are usually thought of as laid-back celebrations, you can you can jazz up your wedding with formal wear and elegant adornments. If you want to make a church ceremony more casual, consider seeking simple centerpieces and allowing your wedding party to dress in a casual style.

## Resorts with Wedding Packages

Purchasing a wedding and honeymoon package together in a bundle through a large lodging facility is becoming increasingly common for people planning weddings on Trinidad and Tobago. All-Inclusive resorts are popular throughout Trinidad and Tobago, and these resorts practically all feature wedding packages.

Booking a wedding package at a Trinidad and Tobago resort is a simple way to organize your big day, because virtually everything is addressed for you. Most packages consist of the following:

Personalized wedding consultant and planner

- Wedding location
- Reception venue
- Officiant
- Floral bouquet and boutonnière
- Cake
- Reception food and beverages
- Photographer
- Marriage certificate

- Government fees

Optional add-ons might include:

- Accommodations for the wedding party
- Videography
- Music and entertainment
- Wedding favors
- Honeymoon package
- Planned expeditions and activities for wedding party and guests

Most wedding packages at resorts on Trinidad and Tobago start at around $1500(USD) and increase from there, based upon add-ons and number of guests.

RESORTS WITH WEDDING PACKAGES ON TRINIDAD AND TOBAGO

| Resorts | Location | Phone Number |
|---|---|---|
| Anise Resort and Spa | Trinidad | 868-670-4436 |
|  |  | 868-670-4437 |
| Cara Suites Hotel | Trinidad | 868-659-2271 |
|  |  | 868-659-2272 |
| Cascadia Hotel | Trinidad | 868-623-4208 |

| | | |
|---|---|---|
| Coco Reef Resort | Tobago | 868-639-8571 |
| Crews Inn | Trinidad | 868-634-4384 |
| | | 868-634-4385 |
| Crowne Plaza Hotel | Trinidad | 877-2-CROWNE |
| Grafton Beach Resort | Tobago | 877-78-HOTEL |
| Hyatt Hotel | Trinidad | 868-623-2222 |
| Normandie Hotel | Trinidad | 868-624-1181 |
| Kapok Hotel | Trinidad | 868-622-5765 |
| Marriott Hotel | Trinidad | 868-627-5555 |
| Seahorse Inn | Tobago | 868-639-0686 |
| Speyside Inn | Tobago | 868-660-4341 |
| Stonehaven Villas | Tobago | 868-639-0361 |

Plan to host your special day on Trinidad and Tobago, and you'll be planning to create memories that will last you a lifetime. From playful beach side weddings to elegant ceremonies held in churches, the various venues offered throughout Trinidad and Tobago promise to provide the ideal location for any couple's wedding.

# Requirements & Traditions

## Weddings Traditions and Requirements on Trinidad
**Saying "I do" on Trinidad on Tobago is as easy as one, two, three . . . days, that is**

The simple process of obtaining a marriage license on Trinidad and Tobago is quite enticing when one considers the hoops some of the other Caribbean islands require you to jump through in order to wed in their country.

You may find that as you learn about the wedding traditions of Trinidad and Tobago, that they speak to you, and that you would like to borrow from the island's customs during your own ceremony. Regardless, there are a few legal matters that must be taken into account before you may exchange vows on the island.

### Local Wedding Customs

Weddings on Trinidad and Tobago are colorful and raucous events. On the islands, the groom is expected to wear a three-piece-suit with a tail and topped off with a top hat. The bride wears a satin dress in white or another pale color such as pink or yellow. Unlike some other Caribbean islands, a processional of groomsmen, bridesmaids, and a flower girl is common here.

After the ceremony, the bride, groom, and their guests parade through the streets to the reception site. Not only do they walk, but they boisterously dance and sing the whole way.

As can be expected, the reception is a lively event filled with steel pan music, dancing, gifts given to the bride and groom, and joyful toasts. Food at the reception ranges from dumplings and crab to Indian *rotis*. The cake is, a spiced fruit cake soaked in rum, is traditionally carried in on the head of a guest, and is covered by mosquito net.

Though these practices may seem outdated to some, they are done in good spirits, and can add a sense of fun to your wedding should you choose to incorporate some of them into your special day.

**Modern Requirements**

After being on the island for three days, couples may apply for a special marriage license at the Inland Revenue Department in Scarborough. The license will cost $55(USD), and can be obtained after the following documents are submitted:

- Original or notarized copy of the divorce certificate if either party has been divorced.
- Death certificate, if either party has been widowed.
- Proof of any name changes.
- Passport.

If everything is in order, the special license will be issued to the couple on the spot, and they may wed after 24 hours has passed.

Whether you choose to incorporate Trinidad and Tobago traditions into your ceremony and reception, or follow your own design path, the beauty and ambiance of the islands are sure to enhance every moment of your big day.

## Why Not Go to Trinidad?

Whether you prefer the excitement of the city, or the quiet of the country, Trinidad and Tobago have you covered

Some people are happiest in a fast-paced city with never-ending attractions that allow them to go, go, go; others prefer peace, quiet, and nature untouched by human hands. The dual island nation of Trinidad and Tobago is the perfect destination for either type of traveler, acting as the figurative "city mouse" and "country mouse" of the Caribbean.

| TRINIDAD AND TOBAGO: FACTS AT A GLANCE | |
|---|---|
| Currency | The official currency of Trinidad and Tobago is the Trinidad and Tobago Dollar (TT$). Occasionally, vendors in Port-of-Spain will accept U.S. and Canadian currency, but it is safer and wiser to convert your currency. In all cases, British pounds should be converted. |
| Electricity | Electric systems on Trinidad and Tobago are not uniform; the most commonly used are the 110-volt or 230-volt systems, but ask your hotel in advance in order to prepare. |

| | |
|---|---|
| GDP Per Capita | The average per capita income is $25,400(USD) per year. |
| Island Size | The islands share about 1,979 square miles in land area. |
| Language | English is the official language, but French, Hindi, Spanish, and Chinese speakers abound in this country. |
| Population | 1,337,684 people call these islands home; 383,100 visitors pass through annually, with 31 percent coming from the U.S. |
| Entry Requirements | All visitors, including those from the Caribbean, are required to show a valid passport and ongoing or return tickets upon arrival on Trinidad and Tobago. Visas are not necessary for visits shorter than six weeks. You will be given a carbon copy of the immigration card that you fill out on arrival, and will be asked to return it upon your departure, so hold on to it! |

## Geography and Weather

Trinidad and Tobago are the southernmost islands of the West Indies, and stand approximately 20 miles apart from one another. They have a total area of 1,981 square miles, with Tobago encompassing only six percent of the total area. Both islands are volcanic in origin, mountainous, and extremely fertile.

Trinidad and Tobago are famed for their variety. The racial diversity in this country is due to its historical role as a main port for the British colonies in the West Indies. Nearly every former British colony, from

South Africa to South India, is now represented in this melting pot of the Caribbean. The mix of cultures leads to a distinct flavor in mannerisms, dress, language, and way of life that is a hybridization of the many people who once moved across oceans to these small islands. Trinidad and Tobago have successfully combined Indian food, African dress, Caribbean calypso and steel-drum music, British English, and the distinctly English love of the sport of cricket into one exciting culture.

Trinidad and Tobago are the closest Caribbean islands to the equator, and have a tropical climate. Average annual temperatures range from 72 to 84 degrees Fahrenheit, with trade winds cooling the coastline. Rainfall is the largest indicator of seasonal change. During the wet season, from June to December, the islands get about 40 inches of rain each year.

**Around the Islands**

Trinidad is the more populous of the two islands, and a more energetic destination. The people of Trinidad are a lively group who like to have fun which may explain why steel pan music and the Limbo came from the island. The traveler who likes to get up and go will feel most at home here, with dance clubs, open air markets, and calypso tents being some of the most popular attractions. Festivals are extremely popular on the islands, and visitors will likely find an exciting event going on during their travels. The most well known festival is known as Carnival. Spectators at Carnival will be treated with dance-worthy musical performances, tantalizing island food and many other cultural festivities. Vacationers will be interested to learn that these islands are the birthplace of tropical staples like calypso music, steel drum bands and the infamous limbo dance. However, rich culture and heritage are not limited to festive music on Trinidad. Some sites worth visiting include the National Museum and Art Gallery, the Botanical Gardens, and Fort Chacon. Click here to read more about landmarks on Trinidad and Tobago.

On the flip side, Tobago offers a quieter, more natural atmosphere. The island has won several awards for eco-tourism, and is even considered by many to be the number one eco-tourism island in the Caribbean. Tobago is home to the Western Hemisphere's oldest protected forest, many secluded beaches, nature trails, bird watching sites, and a colorful coral reef that divers can't get enough of. Nature enthusiasts will be impressed by the extensive avian sighting opportunities that can be enjoyed on the islands; Trinidad boasts more resident species than any other destination in the Caribbean. Additionally, many historic plantations have been converted into nature preserves, providing a great opportunity to learn about the island's history, culture, and nature all at once. Sites you won't want to miss out on include Aripo Caves and Savannah, Devil's Woodyard, and Maracas Waterfall.

When choosing an ideal accommodation during your trip to Trinidad and Tobago, you will find that there are a variety of different options available. Whether you're working on a tight budget, or are indulging in a lavish vacation, the islands offer something for everyone. provide everything needed to complete a perfect island getaway within a single package. Those traveling in a group or with a large family should consider that will make you feel at home, like villas and apartments. Those with an adventurous spirit may enjoy spending their evenings camping on the island, although it is recommended that tourists hire guides to lead them through the island vegetation. Read on Eco Tourism for more about camping and eco-tourism. With so many options, it's easy to find the best Trinidad and Tobago lodging facility to suit your needs.

One thing both islands have in common is their undeniably beautiful beaches. The clichéd image of crystal clear waters and white sand beaches are a reality on Trinidad and Tobago, offering vacationers the picture-perfect beach-going experience they dream about when planning a trip to the Caribbean. There are 10 beaches in Tobago, and more than 20 on Trinidad, each with their own purpose. Some beaches are more suitable for beach combing, while others offer more inviting surf.

**Eat Up!**

After a thrilling day spent exploring the island's cultural and natural glory, travelers are sure to build up a demanding appetite. Given the high volume of tourists that flock to Trinidad and Tobago from around the world, the islands have adapted to the multicultural tastes of travelers and provide a selection of restaurants that cater to different tastes, such as American-style dishes, Asian-influenced fare and more. However, a true island getaway is incomplete without a sampling of the local food favorites. One of the most popular dishes is 'Shark and Bake', which consists of fried dough sandwiching golden morsels of fried shark meat. Other favorites include Callaloo soup, curried roti wraps, fresh seafood from the ocean and rivers, edible roots and more. For a unique dessert, try the Trinidadian version of snow cones. These frozen treats feature shaved iced drizzled with kola and condensed milk. Whether you choose to feast on locally influenced fare or more comfortable Continental dishes, your palette is sure to be pleased with the culinary offerings of Trinidad and Tobago.

**Health and Safety**

Tobago is generally safer than Trinidad, where Port-of-Spain has the petty crime problem of major metropolitan areas such as New York or London. Avoid Port-of-Spain at night, as streets get deserted very quickly. Also avoid evening travel around Wilson Street and the Market of Scarborough, two particularly questionable areas. Always be wary of potential pick-pockets, especially during Carnival, and never leave valuables unattended. Stick to bottled water on the islands.

If you are planning a trip to the Caribbean, consider Trinidad and Tobago, where you can travel back and forth between the islands and feel as though you are experiencing two very different types of vacations. Relax on the beach one day, party the next, and explore the forest the day after that. The possibilities are endless. One of the best elements of the tropical spirit felt on these islands is the fact that foreign travelers are not known here as 'tourists,' but instead are embraced as 'visitors.'

www.ingramcontent.com/pod-product-compliance
Lightning Source LLC
Chambersburg PA
CBHW021054080526
44587CB00010B/244